HEARTBREAK

to HOPE

in the HOME

The amazing story of
Thomas Martin

Guilt, Grace and the Gospel

Heartbreak to Hope in the Home

ISBN 978-1-905989-20-1

Published by
Lisburn Free Presbyterian Church

Printed by: J C Print Limited
Email: info@jcprint.net

Contents

Preface

Do you believe in miracles? I do. I believe in miracles because I believe in God. We serve the God Who can open blinded eyes, heal broken lives and even raise the dead. There is nothing too hard for Him. He is the Almighty God of heaven.

I believe that the greatest miracles are miracles of grace. They are even greater than the miracles of glory. When Jesus Christ stilled the great storm on Galilee He displayed His glory. When He transformed the life of a convicted terrorist like Thomas Martin Jesus Christ demonstrated His amazing grace.

Miracles of grace come at a greater price than the miracles of glory. When Jesus Christ created the universe He did so by the word of His power. Likewise, Jesus Christ's word of command was sufficient for wind and the waves to obey the voice of their mighty Creator. However, it took much more than the Creator's word to redeem and justify a sinner. The awful price of our sin paid in the agony and blood of our Redeemer at Calvary.

Thomas Martin is a miracle of grace and a monument of God's mercy. This story will warm and bless the hearts of thousands. It will also be an encouragement to parents who may be tempted to lose heart and cease praying for their wayward children.

I trust that this book will have a wide distribution and a life changing effect on all who read it.

Victor Maxwell

Chapter 1

Living A Lie

Thomas Martin's phone rang. He immediately recognised his brother's voice, "Hello, Thomas? Colin here. I have a question for you. You know how our mother's name was Corbett, Maureen Corbett? Well, I have just received a birth certificate from the Registry Office in Nottingham and they have put my mother's name down as Maureen Flannigan. How's that? There must be some mistake."

"Flannigan?" Thomas questioned. "I've never heard of it. Are you sure that's right? Sure our mother's name was Corbett, Maureen Corbett," Thomas affirmed. "There has got to be a mistake somewhere. What are you getting a passport for anyway?"

"Angela and I have never been outside the United Kingdom before so we have never needed a passport. If I had known it was going to give all this bother we might have settled for going back to Portrush again."

Colin and his wife had decided to treat their young children to a family holiday in Spain's sunny Costa Brava. They thought it would be a welcome change from the sporadic day-trips to Newcastle or Portrush during the school summer holidays. Too often these outings had been complete washouts due to the inclement Ulster weather. This prompted Colin to venture in search of the sun abroad.

He knew this meant they each needed a passport so he promptly started the application process for the whole family. This meant filling out application forms and answering what seemed like a countless number of questions. Along with the completed forms and a hefty fee, they had to provide birth certificates to accompany their applications. Colin did not have his birth certificate so he had to fill out even more forms for the Births and Marriages Registry. He sent these to the office in Nottingham where he was born. He thought it would be a mere formality, and it was, but when the birth certificate arrived it left him a little puzzled.

Colin was the eldest son of Tommy Martin. Thomas and David were his two younger brothers. He was aware that his mother and father had never been married, but the three brothers assumed their father's surname. Their mother's name was Maureen Corbett, and they had been told that she had died many years earlier.

In light of this Colin recommended, "Thomas, why don't you go ahead and apply for a birth certificate to see what happens?"

"Yea, maybe I'll just do that," said Thomas. The two brothers laughed at the thought of Colin having the surname Flannigan on his birth certificate. Thomas continued, "Maybe someone is trying to wind you up, Colin? Flannigan? It could be one of the lads down at the Orange Lodge taking a hand out of you knowing how strong an Orangeman you are."

Colin soon discounted any such wind-up for he could see that the certificate was authentic and could not have been adjusted as a prank. Furthermore, the certificate was issued in Nottingham where no one even knew Colin. Trying to find out what was going on Thomas and Colin decided to tell their other brother David and ask him to apply for his birth certificate also.

Thomas lost no time in writing to the Registry Office in Nottingham and applying for his birth certificate. When it arrived a few days later it only added to the intrigue. His mother's name was also registered the same as that of Colin; Maureen Flannigan. The ambiguity deepened even more when they discovered that David's document stated that his mother's name was registered as Maureen Corbett.

When Thomas and Colin heard there was a difference in David's certificate they were thrown into further confusion. Colin even suggested that perhaps he and Thomas might not be David's full brothers. They lamented that their father, Tommy Martin, had died just a few years earlier for he was the one who would be able to help them solve this mystery. Thomas said there was only one thing to do, "We need to talk to Aunt Eva and see if she can sort this out for us."

Aunt Eva, their father's half-sister, had been a stand-in mother for the Martin boys since they arrived in Lurgan from

Nottingham more than thirty years earlier. She was always on hand to help her brother Tommy and her three nephews over the many hurdles they faced throughout the years. The boys were certain she would be able to sort this out for them.

When they told Aunt Eva about the inconsistencies between the birth certificates she did not seem to be surprised. The two brothers were taken aback at her casual reaction. It was then that it began to dawn on them that maybe this was not a clerical error at the Registry Office. There was something they did not know, and they were determined to get answers. Eva told them that there was a valid reason for the discrepancy in their names, but she was not able to give a full explanation. She suggested they speak to Agnes Boal since she was aware of the full story.

"The full story? What is the *full story*?" Thomas, Colin and David wanted to know.

The three Martin boys were aware that their family background was very mixed up, and that their childhood home had been far from happy. Tommy and Maureen set up home in Nottingham, England and had three children in quick succession. Both parents were chronic alcoholics and their home became a virtual caldron of hotly contested arguments, violent fights and never-ending nagging ever since the boys could remember.

Just the mention of the name Nottingham usually conjures up thoughts of the folk hero Robin Hood and his band of merry men roaming through the glades of Sherwood Forest. Whether he was sharp shooting with his bow and arrow or skilfully wielding his gleaming sword, Robin Hood was famous for championing the cause of the poor and freeing captives from the tyranny of their oppressors.

Sadly, no such hero was on hand in Nottingham in the late twentieth century to emancipate Thomas Martin and his brothers when they were born into this extremely dysfunctional family. They never found any relief from the constant tyranny resulting from the drunken sprees that were all too common in their home which was bereft of any family love or care.

Tommy Martin, their father, was a soldier with the Territorial Army and gave as much abuse as he took. The relentless contention came to a climax one day when Tommy abruptly decided to snatch the three boys from their mother, abandon their Nottingham home and head back to Northern Ireland. This sudden fracture of the home threw the boys into further confusion and despair. Out of the blue they were uprooted from everything and everyone they had ever known. Before they knew it, they found themselves on their way to Liverpool to catch the ferry across the Irish Sea to Belfast.

The three young Martin boys were bewildered as they huddled together on the boat's indoor seating deck for the overnight sailing. Other passengers were seated nearby while others milled around the ship's corridors. Tommy Marin left strict instructions with his three boys not to move from where they were sitting and threatened, "If you make a move away from here the Captain will come and throw you all overboard."

Overcome with fear and a sense of insecurity Colin, Thomas and David did not budge from the spot where their father left them. Meanwhile, Tommy went off to the bar to drown his rage and guilt at abandoning his Nottingham home and to satisfy his insatiable addiction to liquor. He spent most of the night knocking back glass after glass of spirits. When he returned to look for his boys, all three were still on the same seats curled up and fast asleep.

Colin, Thomas and David had never been to Ireland before. They had often heard their mother and father talk of the good times back home, as they called it. At other times their remarks were not too complimentary about life in Ulster.

Once their boat docked in Belfast, Tommy and his three sons travelled by bus to the town of Lurgan, about twenty-five miles from the city. Soon they arrived at the Martin family home at Ardmore on the outskirts of Lurgan and on the edge of Lough Neagh, the largest fresh water lake in the British Isles. Here they were introduced to their paternal grandparents and other members of the Martin family who until then were complete strangers to the three boys. With this a new chapter in their lives began.

David was eager to be introduced to Agnes Boal, who would be able to help them unravel the mystery of their mother's surname. Apprehensively David phoned Mrs Boal and during the course of their lengthy conversation she explained, "What I am about to tell you is already known by most of our family, but it was never disclosed to you earlier because your dad and some in the family thought you had already suffered enough trauma while growing up and that you should not be exposed to any further unnecessary heartache. Your Dad definitely did not want you to know, and he went to his grave without telling you."

"I can hardly believe that," answered David. "What did he not want us to know?"

Agnes continued, "First let me assure you that all three of you are brothers. There's no doubt about that. When your mother was a baby she was adopted by a family from West Belfast. They registered her under their family name which was Flannigan. That's where she got this surname. As a young adult her name was changed to Corbett which was used on your birth certificate. For some unknown reason she registered Colin and Thomas under Flannigan. However, all three of you are definitely brothers and Tommy Martin was your father."

David was stunned with all that he heard. He had no idea that his mother had such a tangled past. He was also a little uneasy to learn that his mother's surname was originally Flannigan, and that she had been raised in West Belfast. However, this was not all -- more was to come.

Agnes went on, "There's more. I know this will surprise you, but Maureen Corbett, your mother, is not dead. She is alive."

"Not dead?" exclaimed David. It hit him like a thunderbolt. "You mean we have been living a lie for all these years? For nearly thirty-five years we have believed that our mother was dead and now you say she is alive. Where is she? Colin always maintained that our mother wasn't dead. I know that when our father had a drop of drink on him he would blurt out that Maureen was still alive, but we put that down to his drunken stupor. Colin and Thomas will be gutted when they hear what you are telling me now."

David then directed another question to Agnes, "Do you think we could meet Maureen? Would she be willing to meet us?"

Agnes assured David, "I know your mother would be glad to meet you. She has wanted to make contact with you for several years. She lives here in Northern Ireland. I'll get the address for you."

David thanked Agnes for the startling information and hastily made arrangements to relay all these details to Colin and Thomas.

When David told his brothers about his long conversation with Agnes they were astounded and bewildered. Thomas could not take it in and said, "I can't believe this. For years we used to hear Dad spouting about Maureen being alive when he was drunk, but I always put it down to the booze in him."

Colin spoke up and said, "You remember our father's mates used to tease us about our mother still being alive when they got angry with Dad, but he always maintained they were talking nonsense."

Thomas knew that when Colin became a little intoxicated he would also say that their mother was still alive, but he put it down to gibberish because he was the worse for drink.

"It's true," emphasized David. "And furthermore, Agnes says that Maureen is living here in Northern Ireland. She's married and has a family."

Thomas Martin felt gutted. It began to dawn on him that for thirty-five years he had believed a lie. His father had lied and he had trusted him. Now he could hardly take in what he was hearing. At the same time, he began to reason with David and Colin, "I think I can understand why our father did not want us to know all this. We can remember as children that our home was not a very happy place. He must have wanted us to put that out of our minds. It is just a pity he is not here so we could ask him a few more questions and find out what really happened."

Although they were still recovering from the shock, Thomas, Colin and David put their heads together to discuss what they should do next. Thomas obtained forms from the department of the Salvation Army which specialises in locating estranged family members to start a search for Maureen. However, David explained that he already had an address and telephone number, and that Maureen and her husband were living twenty-three miles away in Bangor.

The brothers decided that David should write to Maureen requesting a meeting with her. He duly set about putting pen to paper and posted off a letter addressed to Maureen Corbett in Bangor.

A few days later David's telephone rang, "Hello David. This is William Corbett. I am Maureen Corbett's son." David was a little taken aback but the voice on the other end sounded quite cheery and positive. "She got your letter and told me to phone you and say she would be glad to see you and your brothers. When can you come down to Bangor to see us?"

Although he was still a little dazed by the speed of the developments, David was pleasantly surprised to find that William was so affable and accommodating. Their conversation was cordial and easy. After the initial tentative introductions, David related to William why there had been no contact with his mother for so many years and the steps that had led him and his brothers to now wanting to meet with Maureen. He was not sure if William had been aware of his mother having other children before this.

In the ensuing conversation with William, David discovered that Maureen lived with her husband Calvin in a maisonette on the Belfast side of Bangor. They had two daughters also, Emma and Patricia. David also learned that Maureen had shown no reluctance in agreeing to meet her three estranged sons. Quite the opposite, William manifested great interest in wanting to know all about David and his two brothers; how they were, where they lived and if they were married. He told David that he knew that he had three half-brothers and some details about their lives. He also knew that Tommy Martin was dead.

David wasted no time in relaying all this exhilarating information to Colin and Thomas. After his brothers listened to David's account of his conversation with William, their bewilderment began to be replaced by intrigue. Not only had they discovered that their mother was alive, they were now also learning that they had a half-brother and two half-sisters, a whole new family. Colin said to Thomas, "To think that all this came about because I decided to apply for a passport. If I had not written to Nottingham we might still be in the dark about our mother being alive."

The three boys acted immediately and asked David to make arrangements for them to visit Bangor in the near future. They contacted Aunt Eva who readily consented to accompany the three brothers on their visit to their mother and act as a go-between.

With the date set and arrangements made to meet their mother, the brothers began to feel a little unease and apprehension about how this venture might go. *How would they feel when they met their mother? How would she and her family react to them?* Their memories of their mother were so vague and a little bit tainted by what they had heard from their dad that they could not even imagine what she might look like.

They were soon to find out.

Chapter 2

A Face To Face Meeting

Early one evening in April, 1994 Aunt Eva came over from Dungannon to meet David at his house in Lurgan so they could travel together in David's car to go to meet Maureen. On their way they picked up Colin and Thomas. None of them were sure how they would react to their mother or how she would receive them.

Thomas said to his brothers, "This is worse than going to the dentist."

Colin and David were quick to agree, but Aunt Eva spoke up, "Now, it may not be as bad as you think. You might be surprised for it could turn out OK."

David did not drive with any great acceleration, perhaps reflecting the pensive mood and hesitation which dominated their thoughts. They spoke to Aunt Eva about their uneasiness regarding how the evening might develop, but they unanimously agreed that there would be no recriminations for the past. They wanted to learn what had happened to their mother, where she had been during the intervening years and how they might be able to build a better a relationship with her and her family.

Their apprehension and misgivings increased considerably as they neared the seaside town of Bangor. David steered his car cautiously through the council estate and soon drew up outside a small, white pepple-dashed maisonette. This was the home of Calvin and Maureen Corbett.

After emerging from the car the three brothers followed Aunt Eva up the short garden path to the house. Aunt Eva rang the doorbell, and William Corbett opened the door to welcome the expected guests. Eva introduced herself to William and then introduced her nephews; Colin, Thomas and David.

Each of the three brothers reticently edged their way into a smoked filled room which seemed quite congested once they all crowded in. William presented his mother, Maureen, to each of her three estranged sons. They were also introduced to Calvin, Maureen's husband, who was at her side. It was a poignant moment. The three brothers, now middle-aged men, stood face to face with their mother for the first time in forty-three years.

Upon first impressions Thomas observed that his mother was a small, stocky woman, and he could tell that the ravages of a hard life had taken its toll on her. He figured that her small stature accounted for his diminutive height and slight build and guessed that she was in her mid-sixties. Her beady eyes were bloodshot and her face was deeply furrowed. Long earrings dangled from both ears and her tinted hair was cut short. Thomas sensed a whiff of the unpleasant odour of tobacco and alcohol as he loosely embraced his mother for the first time in his living memory.

Colin and David followed with their hesitant embrace of their estranged mother. Thomas confessed that there was no emotion or warmth in their initial encounter with the family, not from their hosts or on their part. The situation was surreal. Thomas' thoughts were in turmoil. *Is this really my mother? I should be feeling some love for her. Why am I so cold? Why is she so distant? Should I be feeling like this?*

The tension eased a little as they began to talk and recall the events of the intervening years that had been lost. Colin, David and Thomas told Maureen and Calvin about their careers, their families and their children. Eva also entered into the conversation telling Maureen about other members of the family. Throughout this conversation the Martin boys painstakingly steered clear of any allegations or allocating blame on any party.

When Maureen tried to make some rash accusations about their deceased father, Thomas spoke up immediately, "We are not going there Maureen. We have not come here to make allegations about either family or listen to them. What is over is over. Colin, David and I have resolved that we must draw a line in the sand and try to build a future relationship with you and your family without it being prejudiced by anything that happened in the past."

Calvin stayed quietly by Maureen's side. It was clear that he did not want to join the conversation or enter into any controversy.

Maureen fell reluctantly silent after Thomas had cleared the air about not allocating blame. The Martin boys could clearly see that their mother was a tough wee woman, and just as hard and bitter in her heart as the boys imagined she would be. It was evident that she would have liked to say more, but the three brothers would have none of it.

Thomas enquired about Maureen's two daughters in an attempt to steer the conversation away from these more disputable and delicate areas of family life. She told them that Emma had immigrated to Australia some years previously and was now settled there with her family. William mentioned that Emma made periodic visits back home to Northern Ireland. Patricia lived with her family in Rathcoole.

With seven people crowded into the small living room there was a constant babble of conversation. The visit lasted for more than three hours. They had a supper of tea and sandwiches, but once that was over it became abundantly clear that Calvin and Maureen had purchased a considerable amount of alcohol, obviously planning a celebratory party. As the evening progressed Maureen drank nonstop until she became intoxicated. Worse still, Thomas could see that his brother Colin was enjoying too many glasses of liquor also. Conscious that alcohol had been the downfall of his family and fearing that the atmosphere could quickly deteriorate, Thomas decided that they should leave before Colin became completely drunk and reacted irresponsibly to some of Maureen's bitter jibes about Tommy Martin.

Prior to leaving the Corbett's home that evening Colin, Thomas and David arranged with William for another family get-together in the near future. They agreed that it would be a good opportunity for them to meet all the rest of the family, including their wives and children. William suggested that maybe Patricia, his sister, would come to meet them.

In the light of their initial encounter almost being derailed due to liquor, the brothers arranged with William that rather than meeting in one of their homes, it would be better to have the get-together at a restaurant and try to make it an alcohol-free night.

As they said their farewells that night there was still an uncanny absence of emotion or warmth. It was an odd feeling, for although they had met their mother whom they thought was dead there was definitely no sense of bonding in their relationship. Thomas confessed to Colin and David in the car, "I don't know about you boys, but I found Maureen to be a hard wee woman. It's strange to meet your mother and not feel any attachment to her or love for her, nor did I feel that she had any particular love for us."

"I felt the same," said David. "I am glad we went, but I just did not feel she was part of me or of our family. Her son William seemed to be a more affable and a down-to-earth person."

Eva agreed with the boys but advised them to take one step at a time; "That was only your first meeting. Maureen has had a very hard life, and I know that much of it was her own doing. Your father discovered that quite early on, and if he knew what was happening now he would have told you the same thing."

The three brothers decided to take things easy in the meanwhile and wait and see how things would develop.

Chapter 3

Let Me Tell You The Story

No one knows the story of the Martin family better than Thomas Martin. His life has been shaped by events which took place long before he came to the years of understanding. He takes up the account and shares his story:

I am the middle of the three Martin children; Colin is my older brother and David the younger. We were all born in Nottingham, England, but it was not a very happy home. Although mum and dad came from Northern Ireland they decided to set up home in Nottingham because dad was in the army.

I have heard it said that "Mother, home and heaven are the three most precious words of the English language." That may be true for some, but I knew nothing of these values as a child. Sadly, I have no recollection of any happy times in our Nottingham home. On the contrary, our home was blighted by nasty and boisterous arguments, violent rows, prolonged drinking sessions and two alcoholic parents who showed little or no regard for us, their children. As a consequence our impoverished and destitute home and dysfunctional parents deprived us boys of any sense of security or contentment. I often recoiled in fear when my mother and father raised their voices aggressively and threatened more violent behaviour within the home.

I can never remember love ever being mentioned in our family. There certainly was no love or endearment displayed between our parents, and they seldom ever showed any affection towards us. Our home was derelict of these qualities.

Rather than teach us the real values of life we suffered abuse. I can still remember one night when Dad invited his friends to our house for another booze-up. I was only three years of age at that time, but he encouraged me to drink from his glass of black Guinness with its frothy top. Dad's drinking mates expressed their disapproval of his actions. Within a short time of drinking the liquor I was staggering around the room while dad laughed at me being a little drunk. Alas, dad's irresponsible behaviour left a mark on my young life so that in later years I also became addicted to the liquor.

Although I was only seven years old at the time, I can still remember the day when Dad suddenly announced to us three boys, "I am taking you back to Northern Ireland, boys. Your mother and I haven't been getting on very well lately, and we are going back to live with my mother, your granny, and her new husband, outside a town called Lurgan."

The fact that mum and dad were splitting up came as no surprise for we knew that life was far from being pleasant in our home. However, we had mixed feelings at the prospect of leaving Nottingham to live in Northern Ireland. We were abruptly taken out of school and away from our childhood friends. We had never been out of England before, although we had heard both of our parents speak about it quite often, sometimes favourably and at other times disparagingly.

Father assured us that life would be better for us boys living on a farm near to Lough Neagh, with all the freedom of rural life. There would be open fields and hedges where we could play, plenty of cows and calves to work with, little pups and kittens to play with. The picture he painted seemed to be idyllic, and we were convinced that it would be a lot better than life in Nottingham.

Although dad spoke so highly of where we were going, we had no choice in the matter. He gathered up our few belongings and bundled us into a taxi which took us to the train station. After a few hours we arrived in Liverpool where we embarked on the boat that same night for the overnight sailing to Belfast.

We had never been on a large boat before. We had seen small boats and barges on the rivers and canals of England, but had never seen anything this big. After we got on board father found a few seats for us in the lounge. He placed our baggage beside us and got us settled down for the night. I remember it was a little bit cold so dad tucked my coat around me and told me to put my head down and go asleep. He did the same with Colin and David and then before he left he cautioned, "Don't you dare move from this place or the captain will throw you off the boat. I have some things to do, but I will come back for you in the morning before it is time to go ashore."

Dad left us there. It was not that he had "some things to do". His only plan was to go off to the bar and drink away his guilt and sorrow. Alcohol was becoming an all-consuming craving in his life, and all he wanted to do was to go to the bars and drink until he was blind drunk.

It was a long night for us three boys. Although we dozed off, the throb of the ship's engine and the snoring of nearby passengers did not allow us to sleep very well. When daylight broke Dad returned, gathered our belongings and soon we were being ushered down the gangplank to set foot in Northern Ireland for the first time.

Dad bundled us unto a bus which took us through Belfast and out through the rural roads to Lurgan. Within a few hours we arrived at Granda and Granny Dougan's farm at Ardmore on the shores of Lough Neagh. That day was the beginning of some of the happiest months in our otherwise bleak childhood.

Within a few days all three of us were enrolled at Ardmore Primary School. We were not all that excited about school and study. We were even less enthusiastic when we discovered that we would have to walk a mile to school in the morning and a mile home again in the afternoon.

I still remember that soon after we arrived Granny Dougan insisted that dad take us to Lurgan to buy each of us a pair of hob-nail boots. She wanted us to be well prepared for the long walk to school in the approaching autumn and winter. Never before had dad ever taken us out to buy shoes, and if it had not been for granny's instance he probably would not have parted with the money on footwear. Besides, I was not too fond of those boots. They were not only heavy, they were too noisy. When the three of us were approaching the school we sounded like a regiment of soldiers marching.

I really got to enjoy those treks back and forward to school. After experiencing city-life in Nottingham for my first seven years we took a lot of pleasure in learning about so many aspects of country life on the shores of Lough Neagh. At times this interest got me into trouble. Each morning before we left home granny made sure that we were washed and clean. She knew there would be a morning hand inspection at school before lessons started. Inevitably, by the time we got to school my hands were soiled. Sometimes they were stained with the purple-black juice from delicious blackberries we plucked from the hedges along the road. At other times we could not resist the temptation to slide down a muddy bank and in so doing managed to pick up plenty of the earth under our finger nails. I also thought I was a Dead-Eye-Dick of a shot for I picked up every stone on the road and fired the missile at crows, dogs, cats and any other creature that moved.

Those escapades on the way to school were great fun, but they nearly always resulted in me getting into trouble at the morning inspection in school. I recall hearing the story of the little boy in the queue for hand inspection. When the teacher came to where he was she looked at the hand he had held out and exclaimed, "Where could I ever see a more dirty hand than this?"

Her question was answered when the boy held out his other hand. This could have been so true in my case most days.

I really liked Granda and Granny Dougan. They were so kind to us boys. Granny had a lot of pity for us because she knew about our background in England and dad's continuing addiction to drink. We would like to have stayed with them forever, but we knew that was impossible. Too soon the bubble burst and our sojourn in the lovely Ardmore countryside was over. We had lived there for just over one year.

Our exit from Ardmore happened almost as abruptly as our departure from Nottingham. Father arrived home one day early in the summer and announced, "I am renting a place in Lurgan for us to move into in August, boys. I know you are having a great time here, but it is really too much for your granny. She just can't cope with us all living here anymore."

What Dad said was sad, but true. Having four extra people living with them was becoming an increasing strain for Granny and Granda Dougan. There was hardly ever a tranquil moment in the home when we three boys were around. Furthermore, there was no quiet room for them to relax in or have some respite from our family. Besides, there were the additional daily chores of cooking, washing, ironing and cleaning. It was tiring granny out, and the only sensible solution was for us to move out to our own house.

I wondered what our new home would be like. I knew that it could not beat living in Ardmore, nor did it.

Chapter 4

What Can I Do?

Dad said he had a place in Lurgan, and what a place it turned out to be. Number 34 James Street was almost a derelict house. We soon found that ours was not the only dilapidated house on James Street. Quite a few other houses were totally abandoned.

In 1976 when I was fourteen years old, after a short spell in that first house, dad arrived home one day to announce that we were moving house. We soon discovered that we did not have far to move. For that matter, we did not have much to take with us to the other house. We only moved a few houses down the street to number 10. This new property was not much better than the first. We did not have any immediate neighbours for the houses on either side had been vandalized and wrecked.

However, because this house still had panes of glass in the windows the property was deemed to be habitable, therefore, dad moved us into that dwelling. Another advantage for dad was that this house was adjacent to the Thompson & Rodgers paper factory where he worked. He used to joke to his friends that the new location was next door to his work, and this was good on hangover mornings.

Alas, the change of residence did not alter our pattern of life. Dad still spent most of his spare time and money he could not spare, at the pub. All he wanted to do was drink and was seldom sober. Although we were teenagers, our lives were grim and we struggled to survive.

I guess our new residence could have been fixed up and made quite comfortable, but unfortunately, no one had any interest in doing that. Dad's only interest was the bar and the bottle. Now free from Granny Dougan's restraint, his obsession with alcohol became worse. For Colin, David and me, it was a matter of learning to survive from day to day. We did not find it easy to adapt to living by our wits after feeling so contented and secure for a year at granda's farm.

Not only had we to adjust back to the urban surroundings, we were sent to Carrick Primary School in the town where the atmosphere was so different to the more personal and intimate ambiance of Ardmore School in the rural countryside.

At the James Street house we three boys were usually left to our own devices without any supervision. Dad spent most of his time with his cronies down at the Windsor Bar in Lurgan, while we were left to fend for ourselves at home. During the week he was absent from the home for hours on end, and at the weekend we seldom saw him from Friday night until Sunday night, or even Monday morning. That left us free to roam the streets of Lurgan during all hours of the night. We only went home when we were too tired, too cold or too hungry to stay outdoors. The next day would follow a similar pattern.

It was hard to believe that our situation could become any worse, but it did. Often after closing time at the bar, dad invited some of his boozing buddies back to our house for a game of cards. We were quickly dispatched upstairs to bed without any supper. Our bedroom was immediately above the room where they played their card games. This meant that I was able to lie awake and listen to dad and the men argue with their voices raised as tempers boiled over.

One night it seemed that all hell had broken loose. It was already after one o'clock in the morning, and I was just dozing off to sleep when suddenly I was rudely awakened by loud and sharp shouts of anger that were even more harsh than usual. It was clear that things had turned ugly downstairs. The language was blue. Curse words were traded with poisonous venom as the men bawled at each other. The next thing I heard was drunken men fighting with each other. I could hear the crash of chairs being thrown across the room. The table was upended, and glasses were being smashed. It was absolute mayhem. Colin, David and I were terrified as we lay in bed fearing the worst.

The men continued to throw what little furniture we had at each other. The pandemonium was unrelenting for more than five minutes, and then we heard more glass smash. One of the men had thrown a chair through the front window of our house out onto the street. Unwittingly, this man had made our house appear identical to the derelict house next door. Previously, the distinguishing feature between the two houses was that our house used to have glass in the window frame. With the window pane now broken our house looked just as neglected as any other abandoned property in our street. Dad was in no hurry to have the broken window replaced so a piece of cloth was hung over the opening in a vain attempt to keep the wind, rain and cold out.

One day after the riot in our home while I was sitting on one of the crudely-repaired chairs I noticed the shadow of someone trying to look through the hole in the window pane. It was a woman. I asked her if she was looking for anything in particular. My voice startled her. "Sorry son," she said, "I didn't think anyone was living here." With that she hurried away after discovering that our house was not as empty as she had previously thought or even hoped.

It is a wonder that we survived our childhood. When our father was on a drinking binge he seldom bought food for us. Every spare penny went to feed his reckless addiction to drink. At times our hunger was so acute that we resorted to eating sugar straight out of the packet. When we were able to coax dad for a few shillings we bought a loaf of bread and treated ourselves to tomato ketchup sandwiches.

One day while dad was at work and I was at home, an authoritative knock at the front door startled me. When I opened the door I was confronted with a man holding a hard-backed black notebook in his hand. He asked if this was the home of Mr Thomas Martin. When I affirmed it was he said, "I am sorry son, but I am from the Electric Board and have come to cut off your electric at the meter. Your father has not paid his electric bill for months, and that is why we have to turn off the electricity supply."

I did not know what to do or say. Before I had time to think about it I let the man into the house. He opened the electric meter box, tweaked at something and before I knew it the house was in darkness. The man apologised again and then said, "Tell your dad that he needs to be in touch with the Northern Ireland Electric Board (NIEB), and when he pays his bill your electric will be connected again."

After the man left I was perplexed. I realised that we were not only without any light, but there would be no television and no radio. I also feared what dad might say when he arrived home.

My fears were not unfounded. When dad came in from work the house was in darkness. He tried to switch on the light and when nothing happened he asked, "What happened to the light? Did you blow a fuse?"

I spoke up and said, "No da', a man from the Electric Board called this afternoon and said that the bill had not been paid, so he turned the electric off at the meter."

Father flew into one of his all too familiar rages, "What did you let him in for? You had no right to let him in. Never let anybody into this house. Do you hear me? If I had been here he wouldn't have got over the door. Now what are we going to do?"

I cowered under his vehement rage. Dad was obviously not for paying the bill. I do not know what happened up at the Windsor Bar that night, but after dad paid a visit to the drinking place a man returned with him to our house. He went to the meter box and seemed to know what he was doing. Within a few moments our electric was back on again, unofficially.

For months we enjoyed having electric without any bills to trouble us – much to my father's delight. That is, until the NIEB eventually caught up with him. The authorities took dad to court where he was fined and ordered to pay back the deficit to the NIEB over a period of time.

Colin, David and I will never forget Christmas 1971. I was ten years of age. As on other nights, we freely roamed the streets until very late that Christmas Eve night. Everywhere we went we could hear the glad sounds of Christmas carols echoing into the night. The three of us covetously gazed into shop windows where lots of toys were on display. We were hungry, ill clad and very cold. *Joy to the World* was blaring over the town's loudspeakers, but there was not much joy in the world for us.

We woke up early on Christmas morning and came down the stairs. We knew not to expect Christmas gifts. Santa Clause did not come to houses like ours. Dad was still in bed, sleeping off the effects of his night on the town and that is where we expected him to stay most of the day.

However, we got a pleasant surprise mid-morning when two men from the local Lion's Club arrived at our front door with a large hamper of Christmas food for our family. After Colin received it from the kind men we could not wait to open the basket and view the contents. We spread the goodies all over the floor. Colin suggested, "We had better get stuck into this stuff boys before our da' wakes up." We did not have to be invited the second time. We had a feast of all kinds of Christmas fare and even ate the jelly cubes straight out of the packet. By the time dad woke up we had scoffed most of the seasonal provisions, and he had to scrounge something from the leftovers. For us it was a most memorable Christmas.

Without any supervision from a mother or our granny, we became a law unto ourselves. We integrated into the local gangs who roamed the streets protecting our territory. Near to where we lived was a predominately Roman Catholic area which clashed with a neighbouring loyalist area of the town. We felt it was our loyalist duty to protect our own patch and the people who lived there. Nearly every weekend during the summer there was a riot which had been started by one side or the other. It became very popular pastime for young juveniles on both sides of the religious/political divide to join in the rioting in which bottles, bricks and stones were hurled at the opposing sides.

The annual 11th July loyalist bonfire was one of the highlights of the year. From as early as March we, the loyal youth of our area, felt it was our duty to collect firewood and other combustible rubbish such as tyres and old furniture. We piled these items high at the corner of the street and waited for the big night when we would light the great bonfire on the eve of the Twelfth of July.

Once lit, the flames of the bonfire leapt into the night sky and burned into the wee hours of the morning. We generally stayed until the fire died down after which the ashes would smoulder for another three days or more.

These bonfires were very contentious. Youths from the opposing side of the political/religious divide were committed to thwarting our annual loyalist celebrations. They maintained that our actions were provocative, triumphalist and sectarian. Sometimes they, or even other loyalist gangs, would try to sneak into our patch to steal our bonfire material. This gave rise to more rioting and constant battling and bickering across the political divide.

On Monday afternoon, 7th July, 1975, there was a terrible explosion in Lurgan. I remember that the very ground seemed to shake under our feet. It was followed by an eerie and unnatural silence which was suddenly broken when someone cried out, "That's up at the Carrick School." That was our school.

We immediately took off running as quickly as we could in the direction of the school. When we got there we could not believe what we witnessed. It was a scene of utter devastation. A whole section of the front of the building had disappeared and the school wall was reduced to a heap of rubble. The sirens and blue lights of ambulances and fire brigades stressed the gravity of the moment. We could see that two policemen's bodies were lying motionless in the rubble. They appeared lifeless and had certainly suffered horrendous injuries. We heard that the schools caretaker's leg was been impaled on a metal bar. His condition was serious.

Our group of boys was unceremoniously moved away from the scene by the security forces, but we stayed out on the street nearby until very late that night. The sight of devastation that night has never left me. It haunted me for weeks and months at that time for I could not get away from the sounds, the smells and the scene which I had witnessed that day.

I learned later that the Irish Republican Army terrorists had planted a booby-trap bomb at the school. The explosion resulted in the death of one of the two Royal Ulster Constabulary officers we had seen lying in the rubble. This news made me bitter, and I wanted revenge. I felt there was something more that I could do other than build and burn bonfires. We needed to get our own back on these murderous thugs. I wondered how I could go about helping to defend our cause, but what could I do.

The answer to that question would get me into deeper trouble.

Chapter 5

Elsie, Kind And Persuasive

There is no doubt that the disarray of our house and the dereliction of our lives was ample evidence of the absence of a mother or sister in our home. Our James Street home definitely lacked any feminine touch. However, there was a lady who worked with our dad in Thompson & Rodger's paper factory in Lurgan who took an interest in Tommy Martin's boys. Perhaps it was the lack of any motherly care that prompted Elsie to show a little kindness to our dad's three neglected boys. She recognized that our dad had a few personal problems on top of trying to rear three growing children single-handedly. She felt that his dereliction of parental responsibilities lay at the root of his addiction to alcohol. The bar and the bottle were his escape route from reality.

Elsie committed herself to do what she could to help in whatever way possible and whenever she was needed. She frequently left little treats and goodies at our home for us to enjoy. She also gathered up the few threadbare clothes we possessed and took them home to wash and iron. Elsie's kindness endeared her to us and we became very fond of her. She was genuinely interested in us and tried to encourage us to clean up the house and to dress so that we would look our best.

We did not understand it then, but Elsie not only cared for our social and physical welfare, she was also concerned for the deeper spiritual needs of our family. One day after she had finished the ironing and dusting the house from top to bottom, Elsie stopped at the door and spoke back to dad, "Tommy, would you like to come along to church with me some time?" I am sure she had been planning to ask this question for some time.

As if he was already anticipating this question dad was quick to give a dismissive answer, "No, not really, Elsie. Church isn't quite my thing."

Perhaps, fearing that he was disappointing this kind friend, dad instantly looked over to where we were clustered around our old black-and-white television set, and said, "I'll not go Elsie, but the boys would love to go."

I nearly gagged at dad's suggestion. He was making scapegoats of us to get himself off the hook. Until then we had never any intention of going to church. Religion was not part of our lives. Now dad had put us in an impossible situation for there was no way we could disappoint Elsie.

From that week onwards Elsie called by our home every Sunday morning to take two us to the Parish Church of St. John the Evangelist, in Sloan Street, Lurgan. We did not have any Sunday-go-to-church clothes. All of our clothing came from a charity bag which was periodically left at our home by some kind friends. When it came we dived into the bag to find something that might fit us irrespective of what colour it might have been. We had no sense of colour code nor did we have much choice in the matter. We had to accept whatever was donated – beggars could not be choosers.

We made an arrangement that while two of us went to church with Elsie, the one had to stay at home to prepare Sunday dinner. Preparing the Sunday meal provided me with a way to escape going to Church. Colin and David did not enjoy staying at home alone to do the cooking, but I had no problem being alone or doing a bit of cooking. In fact, I enjoyed cooking a lot more than going to church. I used to give one of my brothers my pocket-money to allow me to take his place in the kitchen. Colin and David appreciated the extra shilling or two and I preferred to stay at home. This plan worked a treat for us all.

Just when we thought we had come to terms with attending church, Elsie came up with another brilliant idea. She said to dad, "Tommy, Thursday night is Boys' Brigade night down at the Church. Do you think the boys would like to go to that?"

Without any hesitation father came back, "Certainly Elsie, that would be great. I am sure the boys would love to go to the Boys' Brigade."

There was no room for discussion. The three of us were enrolled in the local Boys' Brigade that very night. I did not mind the 'BB' as much as the Sunday Church services. On Thursday nights there was plenty of activity with other boys and we were able to play football. That was a big bonus.

No doubt our satisfaction with the BB encouraged Elsie to venture with yet another suggestion to dad; "Tommy, down at the church they have started a wee Youth Club on a Friday night. Do you think the boys would like to go to that?"

Almost immediately dad volunteered again, "Oh yes Elsie. That would be a great idea for Fridays. The boys would love that."

From then on we had to attend the Youth Club in the Church every Friday night. I must say we met and made quite a few new friends at the club. Furthermore, we enjoyed the physical exercise and competition of playing badminton even though we had to listen to an epilogue and prayer at the end. Now Elsie had us going to church three times a week; Sunday morning, Thursday night and Friday night.

However, Elsie was not finished yet. Sure enough she was at it again when she spoke with dad; "Tommy, the Church has started confirmation classes on Monday nights. I think this would be a big help to the boys seeing they are at the church so much. What do you think?"

We knew that our spiritual welfare was not a priority with dad, but he yielded again to Elsie's proposal; "Elsie, the boys would love these classes."

In spite of our protestations dad would not give way and soon we began attending the confirmation classes on Monday evenings. By this time all three of us were spending most of the week at church. Even then Elsie was still not satisfied. One day before our dad arrived home Elsie came round to our house with another bag of goodies for us to enjoy. She also produced a tape-recorder.

We were watching television when Elsie arrived and we hardly took a break to speak with her. However, when the television was eventually switched off Elsie seized her opportunity. She pushed the tape recorder over to us and said, "Would you boys like to sing into the tape-recorder for me? Afterwards I will play it back so you can hear yourselves."

At first it sounded like a good idea to have some fun and a bit of a laugh. We giggled and laughed at the thought of hearing ourselves. The three of us then struck our rendition of Marie Osmonds' 'Paper Roses', a big 'hit' at that time. I must say, I thought we sounded not too bad, but I also knew we would never make it big time.

We soon found out that Elsie was not thinking of our success on 'Top of the Pops'. She had another plan on her mind. When father returned from wherever he had been, Elsie produced her tape-recorder, virtually stuck it under his nose and began to play back our recording to him. After we all listened to it several times, dad seemed really pleased at our effort. It was then that Elsie made her obviously premeditated move; "What do you think of that, Tommy?" she asked with a big smile.

Dad expressed his surprise and satisfaction at our singing and for Elsie's ingenuity. She was determined to make the most of that moment, "I knew they had lovely voices so I thought they might like to join the Junior Choir at the church. They have a practice on Tuesday nights during the winter and I was wondering if the boys would like to go along?"

The pattern was predictable. Once again dad readily agreed with Elsie, "Certainly Elsie, the boys would love that."

I felt I could take no more. I jumped to my feet and protested. There was no way I was going to join the junior choir. "Please not the choir dad, anything but the choir." I was thinking of what my friends at the bonfire would say when they heard I had joined the church choir. "They make a sissy out of you and dress you up like a wee girl in this frilly collar and big long robe."

Colin and David tried to back me up in my objections, but it was to no avail. Our dad would not deny Elsie's kindness or offend her. Therefore, he volunteered us three teenagers for the junior choir. Reluctantly we had to fall into line with Elsie's ploy without any further appeal. On the next Tuesday night we were accepted as fully-fledged members of the junior choir.

Through her persistent connivance Elsie had succeeded in getting all three of us, Colin, David and me, to attend church on almost every day of the week.

Chapter 6

Dressed Up For An Occasion

One day our friend Elsie arrived with another of her manipulative designs for our family. She was set to reap a harvest for her unstinted kindness to us. In 1976 evangelist Dick Saunders and his 'Way to Life' team had arrived in Lurgan for an evangelistic tent crusade. The meetings were advertised all over town and announced at most of the local churches.

We were not aware that besides Elsie being so kind to us she also had been praying for our spiritual well being. Consistent with her private prayers, Elsie targeted dad when he was sober and on his own; "Tommy, would you like to go with me to hear Dick Saunders in the tent?"

That put dad on the spot. Until then he had always been able to fob off Elsie's suggestions and use us as his cover. This time he was taken aback and had nowhere to run. He hesitated before giving a noncommittal answer, "I'll probably go with you sometime."

Not to be outdone, Elsie persisted in her invitations until dad finally gave in; "I'll go but just the once," he said.

We only knew about dad's decision to go to the meeting when we saw him all dressed up and ready to go out. It was obvious to us that he was not going to the pub. Colin asked, "Will we find you down in the Windsor Bar if we need you tonight dad?" We nearly died when he told us he was going to the Dick Saunders' tent meeting with Elsie.

God had been blessing Dick Saunders' meetings and many local people had been converted. The meetings were the talk of the town, but dad had determined that attending the meeting would not change his way of life.

It was a chilly evening and we arrived home before dad so that we could watch the television. When he arrived home at almost half past ten we were still sitting around the television with the sound blaring. He generally shouted at us to turn the sound down or gave some other commands. We were so used to it. I came out of the kitchen and asked dad if he wanted anything to eat.

"No not tonight," he said, "I am a bit tired so I think I will just head on up to bed."

We wondered what had happened to him. There was no shouting, no barging, no drink and no supper. There had o be something wrong with him?

A short while later dad called for us to go up to his room for he had something to tell us. We stood around his bed in anticipation of what he might want to say. He spoke slowly and was very controlled as he sat up in the bed. His face was beaming, "Sit down boys, I have something to tell you." Colin, David and I sat on the edge of his bed. He continued, "Lads, your old man has got saved tonight."

We were stunned and at a complete loss to know what to think or say. We did not even know what being 'saved' meant. We knew that whatever it was, it certainly had made a difference in our dad for his face was beaming as he continued speaking, "Dad, you say you are saved. Does that mean there will be no more drinking and gambling?"

"Yes son. It does," he answered.

Coming from our dad, that was nothing less than a miracle, but it was just too big a pill for us to swallow. Dad's whole life had revolved around betting and boozing. We hoped that his conversion was genuine but were not altogether convinced about it all. Dad said he had no illusions about his own inability to keep himself on the Christian pathway, but he expressed every confidence in the power of God to keep him. Dad further explained, "I haven't changed myself. I could never change myself, but the Lord Jesus Christ has changed me and I am depending on Him to help me and to keep me. I know He will."

We knew this would be wonderful if it worked, but only time would tell.

News of Tommy Martin's conversion spread around Lurgan like wild fire. His drinking partners could not believe it. Not long after his conversion he received an outstanding compensation claim for a back injury to the value of £5,000.00. When news about this settlement filtered through to his former buddies at the pubs and clubs in Lurgan they thought Tommy Martin might now even try to buy the Windsor Bar. They were sure that with plenty of money he would be back to his old boozing ways and haunts. I am glad to say they were wrong. They could not understand it and some did not even like it.

At home we saw an unbelievable change in dad. Our 'old man' definitely had a brand new life. Where once he had been cursing us, now he was trying to guide us. Instead of wasting his money he began to spend his windfall on food, clothes and improving our house. One Saturday morning he even took us into Lurgan and bought each of us a new bicycle; David got a blue bike, Colin's was red and I chose a bright yellow one. That bike was my pride and joy for I never had anything like that in my life before.

We did not understand what our dad meant that night when he told us that he had 'got saved' but now we were beginning to appreciate the effects of his conversion and we thought it was great.

Dad's salvation had a profound effect on me. I was not only thankful for what had happened to him, but I was forced to think about it all. I paid attention when he talked to us about what the Lord had done for him. He certainly had learned a whole new vocabulary which was free of blasphemies and expletives. In addition to reading his Bible and praying every day, he spoke to us about the Saviour and how much we needed God's salvation.

I promised dad and myself that I would give these matters some serious consideration, but at some other time.

The conversion of a well-known 'wino' in Lurgan came as a surprise to our family and neighbours. Some of the residents in James Street had never spoken to our father before. Gradually they became more friendly to him and to us. Until then most of them had been afraid of him because of his drunken uproars. Now they spoke to him in the street.

It was also at this time that I was astounded to discover that there were so many Christians in our area. Some of these had also been converted at the Dick Saunders' crusade. Others were Christians for many years who came to tell dad how glad they were to hear of his conversion.

It was Elsie who made the most telling comment. "Tommy, I have been praying for you ever since the very first day I met you. I have been praying that God would save you and now He has. Praise the Lord!"

Chapter 7

Fire At The Factory

They say that faith that can be trusted is the faith that will be tested. The Bible speaks of the fiery trial of the Christian's faith. That is quite literally what happened to our dad in the summer of 1977.

Dad had been saved for almost a year and people were still marvelling that he had not gone back to his old ways. Sadly, we, his children, had not changed. We were still roaming the streets with our mates, defending our patch and building the annual 'loyalist' bonfire.

Just three days before lighting the bonfire on the 'Eleventh Night' of July we were up in the centre of Lurgan collecting all kinds junk for the fire when somebody shouted, "Look at all that smoke. It must be our bonfire."

We ran just as fast as our legs could carry us and when we rounded the corner into James Street we suddenly realized that this fire was even bigger than our bonfire. Thompson Rodgers' paper factory where dad and Elsie worked was on fire. By the time we got there the fire had become a virtual inferno. Huge reels of paper were burning like towering torches with their flames licking up to the sky. From somewhere deep within the factory building, a gas cylinder exploded shooting showers of burning debris high into the air. Police and firemen were trying to cordon off the area. The heat was horrendous and the smoke was suffocating.

As I stood looking at the blaze I suddenly realized that this fire was going to have a dramatic effect on our lives. Not only would our dad and Elsie be out of a job, but I could see that our house next door to the factory was also on fire. I spotted dad at the edge of the crowd and we ran to his side. He was devastated. His soot-stained face bore white tracks where tears were coursing down his cheeks

He slid his arm around David and spoke dejectedly and yet with a sense of resigned acceptance, "The Lord is burning my past, boys."

For dad this was an enormous test of faith in his new Christian life. Later that night we stood outside what was left of our home in a state of sullen shock. The fire had reduced our house to a smouldering shell and besides wiping out everything we owned, it had also destroyed our precious new bicycles, which had been our pride and joy. We hardly knew what to say to each other or to anybody else.

A well-meaning friend said, "Never worry Thomas, the fellas in New Street have agreed to help us build our bonfire up again before The Twelfth."

I was dazed and detached. I was not interested in the bonfire. We had no home, no bed and no bicycles. Everything had been lost in the fire and I felt sick. A bonfire was the last thing in the world I wanted at that moment. I was repeatedly asking myself, *Why has God allowed this to happen to us? Why has God allowed this to happen to our dad seeing he is a new Christian?*

The four of us were soon granted temporary accommodation in Lurgan's Sloan Street and Hill Street. Later we were allocated a bigger and better house than our James Street property in Trasna Way, in the predominantly loyalist Mourneview estate.

In a sense the horror of the fire and the hassle that followed became a turning point in my life, but sadly, not for the better. It was then that I turned my back on God and all things religious. I made up my mind that there would be no more choir and no more church. I intended to live my life to the full and do what I wanted and when I wanted to do it.

Within a short time of our arrival on the Mourneview housing estate David and I got sucked into a gang of a dozen or more loyalist youths. Soon we were roaming the streets of the housing estates in Lurgan town until late every night of the week. We started to go to discos, indulged in smoking, took to drinking and got involved in fights with other youths. Our irresponsible adolescent behaviour was quickly degenerating and soon we were totally out of control.

Father began to blame himself for our wild behaviour. He knew he had been a very bad example to us for the greater part of our lives. At the same time, he felt the only thing he could do was pray for us, and this he did diligently and earnestly.

Some nights when David and I arrived home in the early hours of the morning we tried to creep quietly past dad's bedroom only to find that he was still awake. I have no doubt he had been pleading with the Lord for his prodigal sons, begging God to spare our lives and save our souls.

In spite of his earnest supplications I followed in the paths of his previous decadent life-style. I started to frequent the Windsor Bar where many of my father's former drinking partners recognized me and honoured me with my father's special seat at the bar. "That was the stool your father always sat on, son," a regular customer told me one night, "so every time you come in here it will be yours."

It was a cruel irony which distressed my father even more to know that his sons were taking his place in the public house. There were times when I also was troubled at what we were doing to our father. It was obvious to us that he was ageing rapidly. I tried to banish the sharp arrows of conviction which tortured my mind; *My old man enjoyed himself to the full for many years and then he got saved. What is to stop me doing the same thing? I will enjoy myself to the full and then I will get saved when it suits me, but not now and not just yet.*

I did not know that this was a very dangerous and foolish philosophy. I never even considered the possibility of sudden death. After all, I was young and more concerned with enjoying every second of my life.

At that time some older members of our gang invited David and me to attend several house parties in Portadown. Initially we were not aware that at these functions there was an unlimited and unlicensed supply of alcohol. Very soon we also discovered that there was also a steady flow of drugs at these parties. This lethal combination of drink and drugs really appealed to us as reckless delinquents.

When we began to frequent a number of these late-night and all-night parties in the early 1980s we discovered that there was a far more sinister motive for us being invited to these functions. We found out that these drink and drug gatherings were recruiting stations for the various loyalist paramilitary organizations. At first we successfully spurned and resisted all pressures to join up. We made all sorts of excuses about our age, not having any money or not having experience in paramilitary activities. However, these pleas were not sufficient to satisfy the local warlords. They told us that age and money did not matter. They would provide everything that was needed.

Beyond our excuses, we also knew that our dad would not like or approve of his sons becoming active paramilitaries. Although our behaviour had left a lot to be desired, we had come to hold our dad in high regard, even though his good-living and praying sickened us at times.

However, in the spring of 1981 the pressure to sign up to one of the loyalist organisations increased in frequency and urgency. At that time ten I.R.A. men had gone on hunger strike in the Maze Prison. This resulted in I.R.A sympathisers taking to the streets in Belfast and Londonderry to cause the maximum mayhem; businesses were being petrol-bombed, vehicles were hi-jacked and burned and citizens on both sides of the community were being killed or maimed.

In response to the increased Irish republican activities the loyalist paramilitaries began to recruit in earnest. They told us they were mobilizing their members for what would be the 'Doomsday Battle', the battle to end all battles. They needed scores of new recruits to help them make the last stand for their 'loyalist heritage'.

In late March 1981 we succumbed to these pressures and answered the call to arms. David and I signed up to join the Ulster Volunteer Force in a house in Portadown. We just wanted to 'defend our wee country'.

As members of this illegal organization we pledged to do what we could to further the 'loyalist' cause. What we did not know was that the local police force, the Royal Ulster Constabulary, had infiltrated our ranks and had been monitoring our movements for months.

David and I began to spend more and more time with the godfathers of the UVF. We appeared more frequently at the loyalist parties in Portadown without knowing that the police were closely observing us. They knew that we had joined or were about to join the UVF. They watched and followed all our movements.

It was during the summer of 1981 that David and I first became involved in terrorist activity. We were not yet fully-fledged front-line, gun-carrying terrorists, but we became part of the support network as drivers and couriers for other activists. We were ferrying paramilitary personnel or their illegal arms from place to place and were serving our apprenticeship in the organisation.

By this time the police had collected a significant dossier of information on both of us and had decided to act. Just before six o'clock on the morning of Monday, 19th October, 1981, I was suddenly wakened by the all too familiar roar of police Land Rovers coming to a halt just outside our house. I could hear the incoherent chatter of excited voices disturbing the morning stillness. It sounded as though a whole army was setting a siege around our house.

I was terrified and all of a sudden my blood began to run cold. I lay motionless on the bed and felt paralyzed with fear for I knew why the police were at our house.

Suddenly there was an abrupt hammering at our front door. I heard dad's bedroom door open and him muttering something as he started to struggle down the stairs. He also had been rudely awakened by the beating on the door, pulled his trousers over his pyjamas and was only half-awake. "All right! All right! I'm coming," he yelled at them from the bottom step.

As soon as he unlocked the door he was overwhelmed by a barrage of armed policemen. "Do Thomas Martin and David Martin live here?" one of the officers shouted.

"Yes, they do," dad replied. He was mystified. "What do you want them for?" he wanted to know.

"The detectives over in Gough Barracks in Armagh would like a word with them," one of the policemen explained. "Are they upstairs?"

Without even waiting for an answer, the leading policeman, followed by another, pushed dad to one side and mounted the stairs. They pushed open my bedroom door so forcefully that it banged against the wall. "Are you Thomas Martin?" he gruffly asked.

"I am," I answered quietly.

"Thomas Martin, I am arresting you under the Prevention of Terrorism Act," the policeman stated.

Then the second officer took over. "You may as well get out of your bed and pull some clothes on," he ordered. "You are coming with us".

Knowing that it would not be in my best interests to refuse their demands, I dragged myself out of the bed and masking the terror that had gripped my heart, I defiantly asked, "I am going with you, but I would like to know what you want me for?"

I got the same answer as had been given to dad a few minutes earlier; "The detectives over in Gough Barracks want to see you about one or two little matters."

The two policemen bundled me out of the bedroom on to our tiny landing where I saw my brother David secured between another two policemen. I was really cut up when I saw the state of our father. He had steadied himself against the wall and was weeping inconsolably while wringing his hands in despair. "You have got the wrong boys," he cried to the policemen, "You have got the wrong boys."

He kept repeating his plea over and over again.

One of the policemen spoke softly to dad with a trace of sympathy in his voice, 'No, Mr Martin. We have got the right boys.'

The two of us were driven at speed through the nearly deserted streets and on to the Gough barracks in Armagh as the police had indicated. On arrival there we were interned in separate cells. The next few days were a blur. I do know that both of us were constantly interrogated for three days. After this we were transferred to Crumlin Road Prison in Belfast. We were remanded in custody, charged with possession of illegal weapons and membership of a proscribed organization.

When we signed up to 'defend our wee country' we did not expect to end up in a prison cell.

Chapter 8

Life Inside

When I stepped out of the prison van in the yard of Crumlin Road jail I was scared. The bleak grey prison building only reflected my inner feelings. The thought of spending an indefinite period on remand shot waves of terror over my heart. I was only nineteen years old and was facing life behind bars. It seemed that this was the end of line for me. I feared I had no future.

David and I were marched inside the building to be allocated a cell. Our first impressions of the old rundown prison were not very good and our initial encounter with the other inmates was even worse. Both of us were interviewed individually by prison officers. They asked me, "Do you want to be isolated or do you want to go to one of the paramilitary wings?"

I was not too keen on being isolated, but at the same time, I did not fancy being on a paramilitary wing. Furthermore, I was not sure what to expect or how I might be accepted by the other inmates. However, for better or for worse, I opted to take a chance with one of the paramilitary wings. David chose to be housed with a different paramilitary grouping in another wing. That meant that the two of us were separated from each other; David went to 'A' Wing while I was detained in 'C' Wing.

I will never forget the creeping sense of evil that came over me when I was marched over to 'C' Wing. This was something I had never encountered in my life before. It reminded me of what I had read about Christians being imprisoned and thrown to the lions. When I got to 'C' Wing it was exercise time and all the loyalist prisoners were out in the prison yard. The prison officer just opened the door into the yard and gave me a rude shunt forward, saying, "Away out there and see if the boys want you or not."

As I looked back at the door banging behind me, three men broke off from walking round the perimeter and approached me. Another prisoner came across the yard to join them. I did not want them to see that I was shaking at the thought of talking with these tough-looking characters. Other prisoners shuffled round the circuit of the yard while taking furtive glances over at me.

Once at my side, the four men fired questions at me in rapid succession. They wanted to know where I came from, which UVF Company I belonged to and who my local commander had been. These men were tough and hardened criminals and I knew they were not to be trifled with.

I gave straight answers to their questions, but was never sure what they were thinking. Their aggressive cross-examination lasted for almost ten minutes. After a long silence the men slowed down and finally stopped walking. One of the four interrogators looked at me and then pointed to the other men, "Ok young fella, start walking with them."

I was greatly relieved for I felt I had been accepted by some of the most ruthless commanders in the prison. The other prisoners also had a few questions, but these were mostly about news on the outside.

After the exercise period had finished I was allocated to a cell with two other inmates. The small room was jam-packed with a set of bunk beds, a single bed, a tin locker, a table and a chair. It was cramped in the extreme. We had to take turns to sit on the only chair or rest on our beds. The only toilet for all three of us was a grey-white pot hidden in one corner. This was emptied once each day when we had to do the slopping out.

Republican prisoners had first use of the exercise yard on one morning and then the loyalists on the next morning. The prison authorities made sure the two factions never mixed. With the other two men in my cell I was on a twenty-three hour lock-up every day.

When we eventually settled down to sleep on my first night in prison one of my cell-mates gave me a piece of timely advice; "Thomas, if you should happen to need to use the pot in the middle of the night, beware of the cockroaches. They come in under the door in droves when the lights go out."

Although I was grateful for that advice, my first few nights in the cell were sleepless. It was in those dark hours that I discovered that the old prison was overrun with cockroaches, some as big as two-pound-coins. I think we should have nicknamed our 'C' Wing as the "Cockroach Corner of Crumbling Road Jail."

The conditions at the decaying prison were so bad that the prisoners decided that since their constant complaints seemed to be falling on deaf ears, they would have to do something about it themselves. During whispered conversations in the recreation room and on the exercise yard, a plot was hatched by which they felt this would force the officialdom to do something about our cramped cells and appalling conditions.

The plan was that on a given Sunday morning when 'A' and 'C' Wings were being brought together for the church service, we would turn on the prison officers before we entered the church and then barricade ourselves into 'A' Wing where we would destroy everything within reach, including the sinks, beds and mouldy mattresses. It was hoped this would force the arm of the authorities to provide better and more modem facilities.

This simple and, as we thought, secret plan was to be executed on Sunday, 6th December, 1981. However, something went wrong. The authorities became suspicious when hardened gun-runners and bomb-planters had suddenly developed a totally uncharacteristic interest in attending church. When the planned date for the revolt arrived, the prison officers had adapted a different strategy for taking us to the church service. They only allowed four prisoners at a time to be taken out of either wing. When these four had been accompanied to and secured in the church, another four were taken to the church.

All through this painstaking exercise the prison officers made sure all intervening doors were securely locked behind each group. By this protective ploy the authorities had thwarted our plans to overpower the prison officers.

By out-manoeuvring the would-be rioters the loyalist leaders in the prison were left seething. Not to be outdone, the inmates on 'A' Wing came up with another plan to be carried out later that week. One evening when they were being shepherded out for recreation they took a number of prison officers as hostages and then proceeded to completely wreck their wing. Some prisoners even climbed out on to the prison roof and from there they began to hurl slates down into the prison yard. At first the rioting prisoners ignored all appeals to give up their occupation and come down from the roof.

Back in Lurgan our dad was shocked when he switched on the BBC Television News that evening. He instantly recognized David as one of the rioters on the roof. Dad was dumbfounded and could not believe what was happening.

News of this anarchy on 'A' wing soon filtered through to us on 'C' wing. The command from our leaders was echoed down the corridors, "Loyalist prisoners, barricade your cells."

We did as we had been ordered. We also clogged up the cell door locks in any way we could and piled all our furniture against the doors so that nobody could get in or out for days. The morale amongst the prison officers was at an all-time low while we were buoyed up.

When the riots were eventually quelled relationships between the prison officers and prisoners were extremely tense. Regrettably, conditions for the prisoners failed to improve in any way on any of the wings. If anything, things seemed to grow worse.

One day a prison officer made a sarcastic and arrogant remark to me. I answered him in no uncertain terms and very soon our verbal altercation gave way to physical aggression. A fight broke out until I was forcibly pulled back from the fisticuffs. I was roughly pinned to the floor and handcuffed by a few other prison officers. I was then frog-marched from my cell to another smaller cell for solitary confinement.

Solitary confinement was to prove even more horrendous than anything I had ever experienced until then. I was placed in a cold cell which was furnished only with a table and a chair. The base of my bed was a raised concrete slab which was covered with wooden boards. At eight o'clock every night a mattress was thrown into the cell and then removed again early on the next morning. That meant that there was no way I was able to lie down during the day. The usual toilet pot was in the corner and this was only emptied at the whim of the officers in the morning or at night.

I was a heavy smoker at that time, but no prisoner was allowed cigarettes while in solitary. I was not even allowed to have laces in my shoes in case I should attempt to do anything foolish.

Those days were long, lonely and ever so quiet. I spent as much time as possible eating the disgusting meals I was offered. I ate mostly because of boredom rather than hunger. Meal times broke up the day for me and helped to while away the seemingly endless hours.

After my first day in solitary I was arraigned and given three more days in the solitary cell. I tried to devise a plan to fill those miserable and lonely hours of four seemingly endless days or I would have gone crazy. My intellectual lifeline was a Gideons' Bible which had been placed on the table in my solitary cell. During those four days I spent long periods reading that Bible, but did not understand or make much sense of what I had been reading. However, in the New Testament I recognised verses that my father had quoted to me and other portions of the Bible that I had heard at the children's meetings and church.

After those four dreary days finally ended I was conducted back to my cramped cell where the other two inmates brought me up to date with all the latest prison gossip. Within a short time I was back into my normal prison routine, but still on remand awaiting my trial and day in court.

The only thing that safeguarded my fragile sanity through those horrendous days was the weekly prison visits.

Chapter 9

The Darkest Days

Three times every week, Monday, Wednesday and Friday, our ever-faithful father came to the Crumlin Road Prison to visit David and me. Whatever the weather and in spite of the difficulties of his ailing health, our dad never failed to come on his motor-bike to see us, his two prodigal sons. His regular visits meant a lot to both of us and gave us something to look forward to. Of course, he always had a parcel for us; a bar of soap, a sachet of shampoo, apples, oranges, or something new to wear. Added to these, he invariably brought two copies of the Lurgan Mail, our local newspaper, which we read from cover to cover.

Dad's frequent visits helped create better family bonds than we had never known before. He visited David first on one day and then he visited me first on the next trip to the prison. By alternating his visit to us he was able to relay David's news to me and mine to him. He also brought us news of our family, our neighbours and friends back in Lurgan. When I was locked up for twenty-three hours each day I was able to reflect and mull over everything that dad had told me.

I must say that dad never preached to me when he came to the prison, but at the same time, I could tell he was concerned for our spiritual welfare and we knew he was praying for us. I remember he said to me, "We were praying for you and David in our wee prayer meeting last night."

On another occasion he casually remarked, "Thomas, when I was up the street in Lurgan on Saturday, two different people stopped me to ask me how you were. Before they left both of them assured me that they were praying every night for you and David. Isn't that great? I think it was very thoughtful of them."

I always agreed with dad even though there was no outright enthusiasm on my part for prayer or interest in spiritual matters. Notwithstanding my coolness on the outside, inside I was more cut up than I could ever tell him. Especially when dad frequently remarked with a smile, "This will all work out for the best. I believe the Lord has a purpose for you and David coming in here."

After he left I would reflect on dad's latter statement and thought it was a crazy comment. I thought, *What purpose could there be in coming in here? How could this work out for the best? Dad must be taking this religion to ridiculous extremes.*

Finally, after a long year on remand, our solicitor told us that our long wait was over and at last and we would soon know our final fate. Our trial had been set for November 1982. It was the first 'Super-grass trial' in Northern Ireland in which a prisoner turned to be 'Queen's evidence' and had agreed to testify against a number of his former accomplices. The judicial authorities had concluded that to save court time and costs they could have a number of prisoners sentenced at the same time. However, it did not work out exactly as they had hoped.

On the day of our trial the court was jam-packed. Twenty-seven prisoners were brought to the courtroom for a preliminary trial in which they would have their charges reviewed. Thirteen of us were confined to one dock and fourteen in the other, with lots of police and prison officers positioned all over the courtroom. The public and press galleries were packed and the atmosphere was tense. The prisoners were boiling with rage that one of their former colleagues had decided to turn tail to betray them and tell on them. Understandably, the turncoat needed all the security protection that surrounded him. If some in our dock could have reached him they would have torn him apart, limb by limb

Right from the beginning of proceedings the atmosphere in the courtroom rapidly deteriorated until it became thoroughly obnoxious. Some uncomplimentary remarks were exchanged between the prisoners and the super-grass while he was giving evidence for the prosecution. The mood became so bad that when one prisoner was being brought back from a toilet break the officer accompanying him put his hand on the prisoner's back to move him forward into the dock. The enraged prisoner bellowed at the officer, "Don't you dare touch me." He then swung a punch at the guard. Total chaos followed this altercation.

At this all the prisoners in both docks rounded on their guards and a full scale riot broke out. Fists and feet were flying in every direction. Police officers were freely wielding their batons in a vain attempt to suppress the frenzied rebellion. Flanked by two uniformed police officers, the judge was the first person to be ushered out of the courtroom in haste. The super-grass was also speedily and unceremoniously hustled out of the court for his own safety.

I was mesmerized. Although the prisoners on the fringe of our dock were fighting furiously, I did not get involved, at least, not yet. The panic increased when one of the police officers started to call out, "My gun! My gun! I have lost my gun." To be truthful, I was quite enjoying all the excitement and wondered if I should become involved in the melee.

Just then my attention was attracted to something at my feet on the floor. I looked down and was amazed to see that it was the policeman's gun. It must have become dislodged from his holster and fell to the floor of the dock. Ironically, the gun had come to rest at the feet of a group of angry and aggressive terrorists who were being tried for weapon offences. I thought to myself; *What should I do? Should I reach down and grab the gun? Maybe that would be too risky?*

My deliberations were brought to a sudden and dramatic halt when a policeman spotted the gun and thinking that I had also spotted it, he grabbed me around my neck. I shouted at him, "All right, mate. All right, I'm not doing anything."

With that, the policeman scrambled to the floor in the mass of milling feet and retrieved the missing gun. It took the police and prison officers twenty minutes to regain control of the whole situation and restore some semblance of order.

The trial could not continue on that day because the judge and the chief witness for the prosecution had left the courtroom and there were no plans for their immediate return. We were shepherded one by one back down the steps which led down to a holding cell. Once we arrived there the door was slammed shut and firmly secured. By the time I was led down nine other prisoners were already packed into the very cramped cell. Even then, the prison officers still brought more of the bruised and bleeding prisoners down to the cell. It got so crammed that we could hardly breathe. Before the cell was almost full I realized that my brother David had been very much in the thick of the frenzy upstairs in the court room. He had not shown up in our cell and I wondered where he could be. Just at that David was ushered into our grossly overcrowded cell. Blood was streaming down his face from a wound on his forehead and he had a real bruiser of a blackened eye.

We remained in that crowded cell until later that evening when the security guards escorted us back to our respective cells in the prison. However, David and two other prisoners were taken away to the prison hospital where a doctor administered several stitches to help close the gash above his eye.

The authorities concluded that their super-grass trial had been a complete flop. Furthermore, we soon learned that their key witness, the super-grass, had retracted his evidence and was now refusing to testify against his former partners in crime.

A few days later, on Tuesday 16th November, 1982, the trial was re-convened. Thirteen of us who had not been sentenced at the previous fiasco in the court were returned to have our trial completed. As we filed into court that day some of my fellow-prisoners looked as though they had been in a street brawl or a traffic accident. Bandages, slings and sticking plasters were the tell-tale marks of their previous skirmish in front of this same judge.

I feared that we might suffer a backlash because of the courtroom scuffle several days earlier. Without their key super-grass witness the judiciary would probably have to claw back some credibility and bring the severity of the law down on us. My worst fears were soon realised. The prisoners stepped forward individually to be sentenced. There were gasps and wails of shock from the public gallery as the judge sentenced each prisoner. Distraught relatives just couldn't believe the severity of the punishments that were being meted out to their loved ones.

When it came to my turn I stepped forward. I could see our dad sitting in the public gallery. With a stony stare he was blankly gazing down in my direction while tightly clutching his crumpled and tear-dampened handkerchief in his clasped hands.

There was a hushed and heavy silence all over the court room as the judge solemnly read out the ruling of the court. "Thomas

Martin, you have been found guilty of firearms offences for which I sentence you to twelve years imprisonment," he began.

After a momentary pause to let the significance of his statement sink in, looking over his rimless spectacles, the judge continued, "You will also serve ten years for false imprisonment. In addition, you have been found guilty of membership of a proscribed organization and for this you are sentenced to five years imprisonment. This makes a total of twenty-seven years. These sentences are to be served concurrently."

I was stunned. My legs felt weak and I could feel the colour drain from my face. Waves of nausea swept over me and I felt I was going to be sick. My head was spinning. I had been sentenced to a total of twenty-seven years which were to run concurrently. I was not even sure what all that meant. I was too overwhelmed by the shock to think rationally.

When I learned that my brother David had been sentenced to thirty-nine years in prison I was thunderstruck. I then thought that I must have got off lightly. After the judge had finished summing up I was meekly led away by my personal prison guard to start my long term of imprisonment. Before going down the steps from the dock I glanced up at the public gallery where I spotted my father. His face was ashen and his eyes were red. He weakly waved to us with the damp handkerchief still in his hand.

I was silently escorted through a long and dimly lit tunnel deep below the Crumlin Road. It felt like an interminable downward journey into the depths. As we emerged from the tunnel I heard the sounds of grown men in the underground holding centre groaning, sobbing and some were wailing inconsolably in despair.

A small door was thrown open and I was roughly shoved forward into a cell. The door was banged shut behind me. I was in a space that was nothing more than a small cubicle which possibly measured four feet by four feet. There was nothing in it, just four cement walls and a cement floor. It was desolate, cold and damp.

I could hear the voice of the prisoner next door. He was the one who I had heard wailing earlier. "What are we going to do?" he cried in his deep despair. "What are we going to do? What are we going to do?"

I had no answers for him. I knew that he had been given ten years for a minor offence. I reasoned to myself, This man is so distressed and he has only been sentenced to ten years. I have been handed down twenty-seven. David has been given thirty-nine years. What are we going to do? What will our dad do?

While these thoughts were torturing me I sank down on to the cement floor and curled myself into a ball as best I could to try to generate some heat. I started to shake uncontrollably. My arms and legs were trembling. The little cell was in total darkness with no light whatsoever apart for a chink of a faint glow from below the door. I was totally frightened out of my wits and was afraid of dying in prison. This was undoubtedly the lowest point of my whole life.

In that dark cubicle I became irrational; *I will end it all. I will commit suicide and take my own life. I might as well take an overdose or hang myself. I will have to end it all.*

These despairing thoughts kept me awake. I began to think of our father who had visited us so faithfully and prayed for us day and night. I knew he had dozens of other people praying for us as well. I remembered that he had often said that it was all going to work out for the best. I wondered how he felt about it now. If I had carried out the plan to commit suicide I knew it would have killed him. He had already suffered enough in his topsy-turvy life and I did not want him to die of a broken heart.

Dad's resolute faith in Christ was being severely tested again and this time it was to the absolute limit. I wondered if he still thought this would all work out for the good.

I doubted it very much.

Chapter 10

Knocking At The Door

At that time, David, another prisoner and I were the youngest prisoners to be given such lengthy prison terms for terrorist crimes. It was only after the dust had settled that I began to understand what the word concurrent meant. My longest single sentence was for twelve years. That is the one I would have to serve while the other two judgements of ten years and five years would be served simultaneously with these twelve years. I also learned that with remission those twelve years could even be reduced more.

Having thirteen of the twenty-seven prisoners sentenced at the same time meant that the Crumlin Road jail was overcrowded. The authorities faced a great dilemma and had to decide where they were going to put us all. The three youngest of us could not be imprisoned at the Hydebank Young Offender Centre in south Belfast because the maximum term which could be served there was for five years. David, having to serve thirty-nine years, and me with a twenty-seven years sentence, meant we were excluded. We were finally allocated to serve our sentences at the notorious Maze Prison, just outside Lisburn.

This top-security prison was reputed to be a hotbed of vice and a breeding ground for radical terrorism.

I first arrived in the Maze Prison early in December, 1982. Tensions between the political prisoners were running at an all time high. Republican prisoners in the jail had just come off the notorious 'dirty protest' and the well publicised 'hunger strike' in which ten of their combatants had died. As result, there was a lot of bottled-up anger and resentment against the authorities.

At that time terrorist prisoners were not segregated in the Maze. Republican inmates had a numerical advantage over their loyalist counterparts by a ratio of three to one. This numerical supremacy allowed marauding republican gangs to make violent attacks on lone and exposed loyalist prisoners. Some vulnerable prisoners were trapped and brutally beaten before the guards could rescue them from the clutches of their attackers. Others were severely scalded by having buckets of boiling water thrown over them. It was fearful time.

David and I had to learn quickly that to avoid being housed near republicans we would have to show resolute dissent from conforming to the prison regime. We were told that in so doing we would be classified as 'non-conforming prisoners' and therefore, would be transferred to the 'loyalist protest wing'.

From the day we arrived on the committal wing at the Maze we stated categorically that there was no way we were going to be housed with any republicans. We began to wreck our cells by hammering on the windows with the leg of the chair and bashed out the spy-holes on the cell's door. This helped us qualify as 'non-conformists' and were consequently sent to the 'protest wing' as we had hoped.

In the 'protest wing' we were penalised by losing certain privileges and forfeiting days on our remission. When I had time to think about this I wondered if we had been wise in indulging in our unruly behaviour. We certainly had not helped ourselves and it hardly fitted in with dad's forlorn hope that "it might all work out for the best."

We were soon to discover that our loss of remission and privileges every month would not compare with the long-term benefits we were to reap because of us being where we were. It was on this wing that we first met several prisoners who would make a great impact and difference on our lives. These men were on this 'protest wing', not because of their misdemeanours, but because the republican prisoners refused to be near them.

There was something different about this small group of prisoners. Although they were regarded as loyalists, yet they were not disorderly or rebellious. When I inquired about them I was told they were Christians. Since coming into the Maze each one of them had been converted.

I first noticed these men in the exercise yard where they joined in a game of football. Before returning to our cells, they huddled together for what was obviously a short prayer meeting. I felt strangely drawn to them, if for no other reason than that they reminded me of my dad and all that had happened to him. I so wanted to tell them about my father and the great change in his life.

One day I engaged in conversation with two of these converts and told them about my father and his remarkable conversion. Even though I was a prisoner and was suffering the just deserts for my crimes, yet I was proud of my dad and all that had happened to him. The two men glowed with delight to hear about my dad and told me how they also had been converted recently. In the middle of our conversation one of the men fired a pointed question at me, "What about you Tom? Are you a Christian too?" There was a sense of compassion in his voice

His gentleness touched my heart, but his question also rocked me back on my heels and pierced my conscience. I was forced to concede a sheepish answer, 'No, I'm not, not yet."

That initial contact with these Christians proved to be the beginning of an increasingly rewarding friendship. Every day at recreation period I sought out some of that group and began to spend more and more time with them. They always made me feel welcome and I began to feel more comfortable and contented in their company. There was no swearing, no smoking and no smutty jokes shared amongst them. Although I was not a Christian, being with them also helped dispel the despair that I had been subject to previously.

My frequent presence in their company and attraction to them did not go unnoticed by these Christians. One day early in 1983 one of them commented, "Tom, we are having a wee meeting to study the Bible during recreation period tomorrow evening. We were wondering if you would like to come?"

"Oh yes, I would love to go," I replied instantly.

Back in the cell I could not help smile to myself that I had accepted this friend's invitation to attend a Bible study. All I could think of was that day ten years earlier when dad said to Elsie, "The boys would just love to go to the church" and how much I had resented him volunteering us. I wondered what he would think of me now voluntarily going to a Bible study. He had tried to talk to me many times about the gospel and my need of Jesus Christ, but in those days I had no time whatsoever for these matters. Now, by complete contrast, I started to become aware of my need of the Lord Jesus Christ in my life.

During the next five or six months I became a regular attendee at all these Bible study meetings. I was greatly struck by how happy all these men seemed to be in their Christian faith and their hunger to know more about the Bible. They talked about subjects such as justification, sanctification, and predestination. I had never heard of these words before. In spite of my ignorance these friends still invited me to join in the discussion, to say something or ask a question. Never once did they upbraid my ignorance or make little of my lack of knowledge. They always welcomed my comments and graciously answered my questions.

The only aspect of my association with these Christians that made me feel uneasy was when some of them occasionally asked me if I had become a Christian. Strangely, I never felt threatened or intimidated by their questions, but it invariably struck deeply at my conscience when I remembered the most consistent Christian I had ever known, my dad.

I will never forget the summer of 1983. Lock-up for us was at half-past eight every evening. Most prisoners passed their time reading, writing letters, listening to the radio or talking to their cell-mate. On the evening of Monday, 13th June, 1983, I was lying flat on my back on the top bunk of our twin cell. Jim, my cell mate, was lying below in his bunk, listening to his radio as usual. I was engrossed in reading a small booklet that one of the Christian prisoners had given me the previous day. I was digesting every word carefully. The booklet, 'Let Him In', written by Noel Grant from Bangor, had a picture on the cover of the Saviour, the Lord Jesus Christ, standing outside a closed door, knocking on the door to gain admission.

The booklet reinforced many of the things I had heard over the previous seven years from my father and from these Christian inmates during the previous six months. The booklet reminded me that I was a sinner. I had no problem in admitting that. It was because of my sin that I had ended up in the Maze Prison.

The booklet went on to tell how the Lord Jesus Christ was born at Bethlehem and became flesh and blood in order that He might be able to die on a cross at Calvary and take upon Himself the punishment for all my sins. The simple plan of salvation disclosed that whoever believed in the Lord Jesus Christ would be pardoned from all the guilt and penalty of their sin and be set free in Jesus Christ. They would even be counted before

God as though they had never sinned at all, and better still, they would be accepted in the righteousness of Jesus Christ.

As a boy I had heard all this before. Dad had also tried to tell me this same story many times. Sadly, I had heard him, but I failed to heed the message. Now I was gradually beginning to see that this message was exactly what I needed.

About ten o'clock that night Jim in the bunk below, turned down his radio and called up to me, "Tom, would you like a cigarette?"

He obviously was going to have one himself He stood up to lift the cigarette tin off the table and opening it, he offered me first choice. Hesitatingly I reached out, "Aye, I will have one," I said.

As Jim lit up his cigarette I spoke softly, "Thank you Jim. That is my last one."

Jim was not stupid. He had been watching me for weeks and knew what was happening. He had come to his own conclusion. He looked at me in the bunk and said, "You know, Tom, before long you are going to be a Christian."

That was exactly what I had been thinking about. I stubbed out my last cigarette and lay back on my bunk once more. I returned to reading the book and repeatedly reflecting of what I was reading. I especially was struck with the words of Revelation 3:20; "Behold, I stand at the door, and knock: if any man hear my voice, and open the door, I will come in to him, and will sup with him, and he with Me."

Just then something dawned upon me that I had never seen before; the fact that Jesus Christ, the Son of God, was standing just outside the door of my heart and life. He was knocking to gain admission, and had been persistently knocking for a long time. I had just never recognized it.

Now I began to understand there had been a whole sequence of events; Elsie, our attendance at church, my father's conversion and subsequent witness and now the input of my fellow-prisoners. All these occasions had been links in a chain to bring me to this place. My greatest problem was understanding why the Lord Jesus would want to have anything to do with the likes of me, a sinful rebel. I had always thought that salvation was for decent and respectable people and not for long-term prisoners. These doubts and thoughts threatened to derail and detract me from accepting Jesus Christ as my Saviour.

It was just then that I noticed a phrase printed in block capitals in the booklet and they arrested my attention; "I WILL COME IN". This was the promise of the Saviour. If I opened my heart's door and repented of my sin, the Lord Jesus promised to come into my heart and into my life.

The pattern prayer printed at the back of the booklet suggested that readers could invite the Saviour into their lives. At first I thought about using these words to form my prayer. It was then that I decided to use my own words to invite Jesus Christ into my life. Still reclining on my bunk, I closed my eyes and prayed silently, but sincerely, "Lord Jesus, I am a sinner. You know I am a sinner. I believe that You died for me on Calvary's cross to put away my sin. Please come into my heart and save me now. In Jesus name I pray, Amen."

When I had finished this simple but earnest prayer, an inexplicable peace and sense of freedom from guilt and sin enveloped my soul. Physically, I was still a prisoner in the Maze paying for my crimes, but something miraculous had happened in my soul; I was still behind bars, but I was free; incarcerated by the government, but emancipated by the grace of God and through the power of the gospel. I was forgiven all my sin and the Lord Jesus had set me free. I was thrilled beyond measure.

I wanted to tell my cell-mate Jim immediately. He had already suggested earlier that evening that before long I would become a Christian. Now I had taken that step I wondered if I should tell him. I leaned over the edge of my bunk to look down, but Jim had already settled down for the night. Although I wanted to waken him to share my good news I felt it was best to wait until the next morning. I so wanted to tell somebody what had happened to me; I wanted to tell Jim and wanted to tell everybody about my new life in Jesus Christ.

It was now near to midnight so I would have to wait until the next morning.

Chapter 11

Tell It Out

When I eventually awoke next morning, Jim was already awake and preparing for the day.   He greeted me with the usual, "Good morning, Tom."

Although I was still a little groggy I retorted, "'Morning Jim."

At first I thought I had better tell him that I had accepted the Lord Jesus Christ as Saviour late on that previous night, but I hesitated and decided I would tell him after I got dressed. That was a mistake. I had forgotten that Jim was an orderly and was due on the first shift early that morning. That meant he had to be in the dining-room half-an-hour before the other prisoners.

While I was still dressing a prison officer came to the cell for Jim and before I knew it he had gone. I felt bad about this for I had promised myself that Jim would be the first I would tell about my conversion. I had read in the booklet that I should confess the Lord Jesus Christ to others and it suggested telling another Christian. I, therefore, decided to wait in the corridor just outside my cell in the hope that one of my Bible-Study friends might come my way. I greeted many of the boys on their way to the canteen, but I did not see any of the Christians I had been looking for.

Finally, several Christians did come by, but when I attempted to arrest their attention and share my news, I froze and let the opportunity pass by. As a result I was becoming more and more frustrated and felt I would never be able to confess Jesus Christ as Lord to anyone.

Just then I remembered Bobby, a Christian who occupied the cell at the end of our corridor. I had not seen him come out of his cell so I made my way to it. I peered in through the door only to find that Bobby was comfortably curled up on his bunk and still fast asleep. Again my plans to tell someone about my salvation were thwarted. I thought; *Who am I ever going to tell?*

It suddenly dawned on me that there was no one better to share my news with than my brother David. He knew all about what had happened to our father and would be able to recall the night dad had called us up to his bedroom and said he had 'something to tell' us. Now I had 'something to tell' my brother.

I asked some of the other prisoners if they had seen David. They told me he had already gone to the washroom. I ran back to my cell to pick up my wash gear and headed off in the direction of the same washroom. I wanted to catch David before he went to the dining room for breakfast.

When I got there I found that the washroom was virtually empty, which was most unusual at that time of morning. However, David was using the middle sink in a long row of basins. I set my toilet bag down on the basin right beside David's. I still remember he was brushing his teeth and frothy bubbles of toothpaste surrounded his mouth. I turned on the tap at my washbasin and then slowly turned it off again. This was my big chance.

Turning to David I seized the opportunity. "Dave, I have something to tell you," I began.

"What is it, Tom?" he asked through the foam of his toothpaste.

I bluntly blurted it out to him, "I have become a Christian."

David stopped brushing and took the toothbrush out of his mouth. He looked at me with amazement and exclaimed, "You have what?"

I am glad to say there was more a sense of approval in his voice rather than displeasure. At last the ice was broken. I had finally managed to tell somebody and immediately I began to feel better. Now there could be no turning back.

I took time to tell David in detail how I got saved on the previous night while still lying in my bunk and reading a booklet which one of the prisoners had given me. I told him I had asked the Lord Jesus Christ to come into my heart.

David seemed to be enthusiastic when he asked, "Have you told anybody else about this?"

"No, I haven't told another soul yet," I replied. "I wanted to tell you first." This I said in spite of spending the previous fifteen minutes trying to tell some of the other prisoners.

"Well, we will soon tell somebody," was David's instant reaction. Although he was not a Christian, David had been greatly influenced by our father. He knew how dad's life had been transformed. Now he wanted to tell others what had happened to his brother. News of my conversion spread like wildfire through the wing, prisoners and prison officers alike.

Later I was able to meet up with my Christian inmate friends and describe to them my experience of conversion on the previous evening. They were thrilled to hear of my conversion. Confessing Jesus Christ to Christians and non-Christians alike, gave me great satisfaction and a real sense of assurance. I felt like I was walking on air. I was sure I had been forgiven and was accepted by the Saviour as a child of God. I was saved and I knew I was saved.

One of the other Christian prisoners quoted a verse from the Bible to me and it described exactly how I felt; "If the Son therefore shall make you free, ye shall be free indeed." *Free indeed*, these two words summed up my sentiments. I was liberated in my soul and had a new life in Christ, as a child of God and the son of a King.

After lock up that evening I commandeered the cell's sole table and chair. There were two things I had to do before retiring for the night; first I had to tell Jim, my cell mate, about my conversion.

Looking across from the table to where Jim was relaxing on his bunk, reading and smoking, I broached the subject. "Jim, do you remember what you said to me last night?" I asked.

"Yes, I do Tom, and some of the other boys have told me it has happened," Jim replied with a knowing smile.

"I was saved last night while I was lying up there reading that little book. Just after you went to sleep I accepted the Lord Jesus as my Saviour." I considered it to be important that I should witness to Jim.

'That's good, Tom, very good," Jim replied and with a mischievous expression he went on, "I told you that it was going to happen."

"Yes Jim, you did," I replied. Before I could say anymore Jim had put his book up over his face again and the subject was obviously closed for now.

My other priority before going to sleep was to write a letter to my dad. The pen in my hand seemed to glide over the page and the joy of my heart coursed like liquid ink unto the page. I told him how God had answered his fervent prayers and that on the previous evening I had come to know the Lord Jesus Christ as Saviour just as he had done seven years earlier. I also told him to keep on praying for David for he was proudly telling others all over the prison of my conversion.

After I had finished this letter I read it over again and as I did so I could hardly contain my emotions. I tried to imagine how it would be when dad would read my correspondence a few days later. I was sure he would weep with joy just as I was doing.

This early joy of my new-found Christian faith made me feel like I was on top of the world all through the next day. I spoke confidently to all my prison friends and told them what had happened to me on the previous night. However, the first real test of faith came four days later when I was confronted with a choice; one of the most popular TV programmes of the week was 'Top of The Pops'. It was screened every Thursday evening at seven o'clock. Many of the prison inmates were avid fans of rock and pop and that included me. I was always one of the first to be down in the canteen to secure a good seat for the Thursday evening show. I was always enthralled with the music, the fame and fortune of groups such as the Eurhythmics and UB40, or pop idols like David Bowie. I knew them all and was always up to date with pop music magazines.

That night I recognised that as a Christian I had a difficult decision to make. There was a Bible study at exactly the same time as my favourite television programme. I would always have been in the canteen, glued to the screen, at that particular time. However, that morning, Bobby, whose cell was at the end of corridor, casually said, "Would you like to come along to our Bible study group this evening, Tom? I'm sure you would find it helpful. At present we are reading a book by Dr Martyn Lloyd-Jones and discussing it together."

His question put me on the horns of a dilemma. "Thanks for the invitation, Bobby," I hedged, "but I don't think I will be able to make it this evening."

I felt so guilty after saying this to my friend. It was as if my inner conscience convicted me; *Not able to make it? Who was I kidding? Where could I possibly be going seeing I was in prison?*

Bobby accepted my comment, "That's ok. Don't worry about it, Tom," Bobby replied sympathetically. "Any time you feel like it you are welcome to come along. We will always be glad to see you."

It was left at that. "Come when you like. We will always be glad to see you," Bobby remarked as he left.

Bible study or 'Top Of the Pops', I wrestled with the choice between the two all day. I was in spiritual turmoil as my old ways and old nature grappled with the new nature which wanted to go to the Bible study. As the afternoon wore on I knew that I had to come to some conclusion and do something.

It was a battle, but by teatime I had made my choice, the right choice. After tea, I saw three Christians going past my cell on the way to the Bible study. Immediately I fell into step not too far behind them. I entered the small cell soon after the three brothers and spoke almost apologetically, "Excuse me boys, would it be all right if I came to your meeting tonight?"

"No problem. Come on over here and find somewhere to sit," said one of the men already seated on the bottom bunk.

"It's great to see you, Tom," another said, with genuine warmth and enthusiasm. "Of course it's all right for you to join us."

After sitting down in the least conspicuous spot I could find, I spent the next two hours with these Christians as we read and discussed Dr Martyn Lloyd-Jones' book about the problems of spiritual depression.

Although I did not understand much about the book or what they were talking about, I found the discussion and study to be so stimulating and inspiring. Furthermore, I felt so secure and at home in the company of these Christians.

I heard afterwards that I was missed by my other friends in the canteen that night, but I was glad that God had helped me make the right decision and the new nature won through.

I never went back to the canteen on a Thursday night. I had found a better attraction in the Word of God and with the saints.

Chapter 12

And There's More

Early on Sunday morning, July 31st, 1983, a little more than a month after my conversion, I was lying on my bunk contemplating whether I should go to the washroom first or the dining hall for breakfast. My cellmate, Jim, had already gone. I opted to go to the washroom first so I grabbed my towel and just as I swung my legs over the edge of the bunk, I heard this spun-out and penetrating shout coming from down the corridor outside, "Halleluuuuuujah!".

I was so bowled over with the ear-splitting holler that I jumped from the bed to the floor and said within myself, I guarantee that's our David. *He has been asking a lot of questions recently and showing a lot of interest in spiritual matters.*

I had spoken with David about salvation almost every day since my own conversion, and earnestly prayed for him every night. I had this witness in my heart that the "Halleluuuuuujah" must be because of David and I was not wrong.

I was so excited that I rushed to open the cell door in the

anticipation of hearing David's good news. Sure enough, there he was approaching my cell with his face beaming. Jim Watt, another Christian, had an arm around David's shoulder. Jim was the first person to whom David had dared to confess his faith in Christ about five minutes earlier.

In the early hours of that Sunday morning David had asked the Lord to save him. When the inmates at the Maze wakened later David ventured out into the corridor to tell someone about what had happened to him. Jim Watt was just ahead of him so David quickened his pace to catch up with Jim and quietly said, "Jim, I thought you would like to know that I got saved last night."

'Tell me again what you said, Dave?" said Jim, pretending not to hear.

David spoke a little louder, "I said, I got saved last night."

When he heard David speak so loudly of his conversion, Jim bellowed the resounding "Halleluuuuuujah!" which had resonated down the corridor and had arrested my attention in the cell.

As they both approached I heard Jim say to David, "Tell Tom the good news, David."

David dropped his head for a second, then lifting his eyes he looked at me and said, "Tom, I just want to tell you that I got saved in my cell last night."

I was overcome with emotion again and just reached forward to put my arms around my young brother Davy. We hugged each other tightly and I wept. We had always been blood brothers, even partners in crime and fellow-prisoners. Now we were brothers in Christ and children of God.

Through my tears I just said, "Praise the Lord!"

On Tuesday morning, two days later, dad received another thrilling letter, from David this time, to tell him the good news. A month earlier he had received my letter telling him of my conversion. Now he had the inexpressible joy of hearing of this wonderful answer to prayer in the conversion of another son. Dad had never given up in praying for his "boys in prison". Now God had answered those prayers in a marvellous way.

Dad later told me that when he received David's letter relating his good news he sat back in his armchair with tears of joy coursing down his cheeks. He had always maintained that the Lord had a purpose in all that was happening to us. That prediction had proved correct. Now he was seeing God's purpose unfold.

Dad recalled how that God had given him a Bible verse from which he had gleaned a lot of comfort through the years. It had sustained him through those long dark winter days and during the seemingly endless and impossible situations. Dad reached across to the table beside him and lifted his well¬-worn Bible and read a verse again, "For perhaps he therefore departed for a season, that thou shouldest receive him for ever" (Philemon 1:15). Dad closed his Bible, dried his eyes and silently prayed, "Thank you, thank you, Lord!"

Other prisoners were not necessarily as enthusiastic about the conversion of the Martin brothers as our dad and the Christian inmates. Some were cynical and wary of all these Christians and their constant 'witness' to the gospel. We were acutely aware that many of the non-believers were afraid that these newly converted prisoners would turn to be super-grasses and incriminate some of them.

They certainly had nothing to fear from David and me. We had found a new joy and incentive for living. It was as if we had discovered a treasure. We met with other believers for personal and collective prayer and Bible study and through it all we were drawn closer to God and to each other.

In late November, 1983, David and I had a strange spiritual experience. One morning before breakfast David arrived at my cell. He said he had something to tell me that could not be left until later; "I know it is kind of early in the day, Tom, but I have something I feel I need to share with you and I felt I ought to do it as soon as possible."

I was dumbfounded, "Funny you should say that, Dave, for I was just on my way out to try to find you. There is something that I feel I would like to share with you."

For weeks God had been speaking to me about leaving the protest wing. As a Christian I felt it was not right to be there and I should not be part of it. I was no longer rebelling against the prison regime. I tried to put this conviction out of my mind several times, but it would not go away. I also knew that to come off the protest might result in being branded as a coward and a traitor to the cause or even have consequences in 'measures' that might be taken against me physically.

I was curious to find out what David wanted to speak to me about. I thought; *It could not possibly have anything to do with what I had been thinking.*

I asked David what was on his mind. "It's just this, Tom," David began to explain. "Last night in my cell I was reading the Bible in 2 Corinthians 6:17 and came upon these words, 'Come out from among them, and be ye separate, saith the Lord, and touch not the unclean thing; and I will receive you.'"

I was already anticipating his next words as he continued, "I hardly slept a wink all last night, Tom, just thinking about this. I believe God wants us to leave the protest wing."

I staggered at what he had said. What I was about to say would also astound David, "I also have been reading the Bible and came on these verses in Matthew 6:24 'No man can serve two masters: for either he will hate the one, and love the other; or else he will hold to the one, and despise the other. Ye cannot serve God and mammon.' Dave that is what I have been doing for a long time. I have been trying to serve two masters; the prisoners on this wing and God above. The Bible says it can't be done."

We just stood staring at each other in a state of spiritual

shock. I further volunteered, "That surely means that God must be speaking to the both of us and now we will have to do something about it."

Leaving the protest wing was not easy. We would have to tell the other hardened prisoners on our block and gain permission from the loyalist commanders on the wing. Over the next few weeks we spent a lot of time discussing the different ways we might be able to be released from this protest wing. Our sense of panic caused us several sleepless nights thinking about the best way to go about this move besides constantly praying for God's guidance and help.

Just after two o'clock one afternoon we were all released for recreation. David and I saw our opportunity in the corridor to speak with Billy, one of the top loyalists on our wing. We were shaking in our shoes, but I decided we would take the plunge and speak up; "Billy could Dave and I have a wee word with you and maybe a couple of the other commanders?" I said.

Billy answered warmly, "Certainly, Tom, no problem. Come on back to my cell where we can have a chat."

Billy invited two other loyalist leaders to join us. Once in Billy's cell with the door closed, the three leaders, one from the UDA and the other two from the UVF, wanted to know what was on our mind "Well, boys, what can we do for you? What's your problem?"

I began uneasily, "It's just like this, we want to leave the protest."

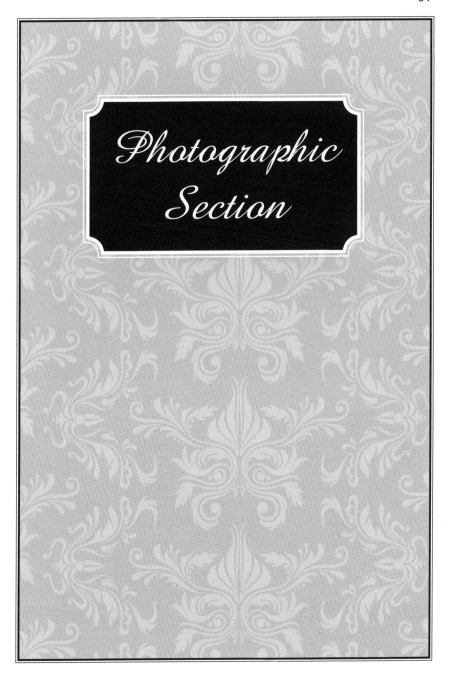

Photographic Section

Dave, Colin and Thomas at Grandma's farm in Ardmore

Thomas (in middle) - James Street, Lurgan

Thomas with a friend in James Street

Thomas on a bike in James Street

Thomas on his yellow bike, his pride and joy. in James Street

Thomas (right), David and their dad in James Street, Lurgan

Thomas in middle. Notice the poor condition of the house. The inside was worse

Thomas (left) David and their dad Tommy

Thomas (right) and his brother Colin with their dog Sunny

Thomas (with back turned) in the choir - love the hair!

One of the many bonfires the boys built for the 11th of July celebrations

Thomas with his favourite dog Sunny in Hill Street

Thomas' dad on the bike he used to go to prison to visit the boys

Thomas (right) and David out on parole

Tommy welcomes Thomas home on parole - what a blessed day!

Tom and June on Tom's first parole

Thomas and June (engagement photo)

Thomas and June (wedding day photo)

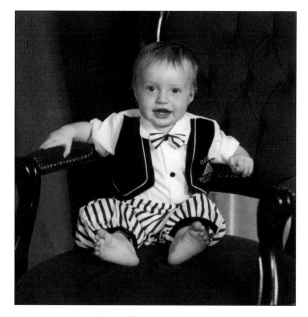

Aaron Then there was one

Aaron and Samuel Then there were two

Aaron, Samuel and Timothy Now there are three

Thomas' mother Maureen (dark glasses)

Thomas , David and Colin

The three commanders were taken aback. Billy was the more experienced of the commanders and had handled many requests like this before. He wanted to know why the two of us who had once been so militant, would want to 'chicken out'. "Is someone bothering you or somebody giving you a hard time? If so, I will be glad to sort it out for you," said Billy.

Although David and I were taking our stand for the Lord we certainly did not feel like we were heroes for the faith. We were scared stiff and afraid that it all might turn very sour.

While David prayed silently, I spoke up, "No, Billy, it's nothing like that. The problem is that we are Christians now and we feel that it is not right for us to continue to be on the protest. We should be conforming to prison regulations. You see, we have a new Commander in our lives now. We want to serve God."

I could hardly believe I was saying all of this to three of the most influential loyalist leaders in the Maze.

There was a brief consultation between the three wing commanders. These men were fanatical and wielded enormous authority in the loyalist ranks. After a few minutes of deliberation, they looked over at the two of us. Billy continued in his role as their spokesman; "We have been watching you boys for months and we know that you are genuine, through and through. You probably don't realize this either, but you have a tremendous calming influence on this wing. We don't want to lose you and we would do anything to help the pair of you, just to keep you here with us. Would you not consider changing your mind?" Billy asked.

We could barely believe what we were hearing. Billy seemed to be almost begging us to stay. When we had recovered our composure I spoke again, "Thank you for saying that Billy, but we are definitely going. As I said, the Lord is our Commander now, and this is a big thing for us."

Billy shook his head before finally conceding, "Well, if that's the way you feel about it, then you may go. We have to say that we appreciate the fact that you have come to tell us that you are leaving. At least you didn't go squealing to the Governor or the prison officers." The other two leaders nodded their heads in agreement with Billy.

All three men stepped forward and shook our hands as we left the room. Billy called after us, "You can be sure, boys, that nobody will say anything to you. And nobody will do anything to you. Just leave that with us."

Both of us felt just as weak leaving the room as we had felt going in half an hour earlier. Nevertheless, we walked towards the exercise yard with our heads held high. We felt like we had been with Daniel in 'the den of lions'.

On the following day we were moved out of the protest wing. Later I was reminded of a verse of Scripture in Proverbs "When a man's ways please the LORD, He maketh even his enemies to be at peace with him" (Proverbs 16:7).

We had proved that Daniel's God is still on the throne.

Chapter 13

Dropping A Line

Life back on the regular 'conforming wing' demanded some adjustments, but after a while the daily routine became just as tedious as on the other wing. We were able to enjoy some privileges that we had been denied while on the protest. Furthermore, we met up with other Christians and their fellowship helped us to grow in our Christian lives.

Frequent visits from our brother Colin and our dad kept us in touch with what was going on in their lives. *The Lurgan Mail* continued to provide us with news of local happenings. However, life 'behind the wire' at the Maze seemed to be far removed from life in the 'real world' on the outside. I often pondered on what dad had remarked when David and I were first remanded in custody, "Maybe there is a purpose in all this and it will work out for the best."

We knew that God was certainly at work in our lives. Early in November, 1985, almost two years after David and I had come off the protest wing, God initiated another life-changing episode in my life.

While in prison we were always glad to receive correspondence from friends on 'the outside'. One person who took a genuine interest in the welfare of the prisoners was Florence Cobb from Hillsborough, whose husband Harry had been killed in a terrorist attack in Lurgan years earlier. Rather than spend the remainder her life in lonely and bitter isolation, Florence had decided to engage in the practical ministry of communicating with long term prisoners and encouraging other Christians to do likewise.

It was in November 1985 that Florence gave the name of Jim Brown, a prisoner whom we nicknamed 'Hovis' Brown, to Gaye Matthews in Lisburn and asked her to drop him a few lines. When Gaye discovered that Jim was a Christian she thought that was a good starting point on which to base her correspondence.

One day Gaye was composing her letter to Jim during the morning break at the shop where she worked in Lisburn. Just then, another shop assistant noticed that Gaye was so absorbed in writing. "What are you doing, Gaye?" asked the assistant.

Gaye replied, with a short laugh, "June, I am trying to write a letter to a fellow in prison. I have never met him, but a lady who arranges for Christians to write to prisoners gave me his name. I know nothing about him, what he looks like or where he comes from. I don't even know what age he is. All I know is that he is called Jim Brown and that he is a Christian."

Knowing that June was also a Christian, Gaye pushed the writing-pad across to June and jokingly said, "Here June, why don't you add a wee bit to the end of my letter?"

"But what will I say Gaye?" answered June with an embarrassed giggle.

"Tell him who you are and where you work," Gaye suggested.

June sat down and wrote a few introductory remarks; "My name is June Thompson. I will be praying for you. My address is: 28, North Street, Upper Ballinderry." June could not think of anything else to add to Gaye's letter so she passed the writing-pad back to her friend.

I knew nothing about this until a few days later when I met Jim Brown in the exercise yard at the Maze. He had a letter in his hand when he called me, "Hey Tom, how would you like to write to a Christian girl? I have the names and addresses of two girls and I think one will probably be enough for me!"

Without too much hesitation or thought, I responded, "Yes, I suppose I would, Jim, it would always be something to do."

Jim opened his letter and asked, "Which one of the two would you like to write to?"

"How would I know? Which one wrote to you?" I laughingly asked.

"Gaye Matthews wrote to me but, her workmate, June Thompson, also sent her address in the letter. Would you like to write to her?" Jim replied.

I agreed with Jim and said, "That's fine, I'll write to the other one. What did you say her name was?

Jim looked at the page again and said, "She is called June Thompson. Here is her address." With that he tore off June's part of the page and gave it to me.

Back in my cell that evening I started to write a short letter to this new but unknown Christian pen-pal. Besides asking a few questions about June I introduced myself and I related the story of my conversion and what had happened in my life since I came to the Lord.

Although I had intended to only write a short letter I had actually written a couple of pages before deciding it was time to stop. I knew nothing about this girl and I did not even know if she would be interested in what I had to say. The thought also occurred to me that this girl might even have a boyfriend and I wondered what he might think of me writing to June.

On Thursday evening, 7th November, 1985, when June Thompson arrived home from work, she was surprised to find a letter waiting for her. June certainly had never received a letter like this before. Twice it had been stamped with the Maze Prison censorship imprint. Notwithstanding that the letter was from someone in prison, June said she had great satisfaction to know that somebody cared enough to write her a letter. I learned afterwards that she also found my testimony to be quite amazing and felt constrained to write again and encourage me. Within a week I had another letter from June to which I quickly replied.

Our accelerated exchange of correspondence helped me to discover that June was a shy and unassuming Christian young woman. Through our letter-writing we slowly built up a relationship even though we had never met each other. I treasured June's letters and at Christmas I gladly and proudly displayed the greeting card she had sent me.

Even more meaningful to me was another card I received from June two days before Christmas. It had bold letters emblazoned in block capitals on the outside of the card which spelt out June's message to me; "THINKING OF YOU". June wrote on the inside, "I saw this card in the shop yesterday and bought it for you. I thought you might be lonely at Christmas. I just wanted you to know that I am thinking of you. June."

I really treasured this card and was greatly touched that someone should be thinking of me.

Over the next few months our letters became increasingly long and more frequent. We began to encourage each other in our Christian lives and share our difficulties and problems. This encouraged me to take the bold step of asking June that if she would be interested in paying me a visit at the Maze if I sent her a visitor's pass.

After I sent the letter I had all sorts of thoughts about what I had done; *maybe she will be too embarrassed to come to the Maze. Perhaps she will think I am too forward or too quick off the mark. Would she want to be associated with a prisoner in the Maze?*

I only had to wait four days until I received a reply to my enquiry; "Of course I would love to come and visit you," wrote June. I was over the moon with her reply. She continued, "Could you make it for a Wednesday for that is my day off work."

I wasted no time in securing a visitor's pass for June. It was all set for June Thompson to meet Thomas Martin at Her Majesty's Maze Prison on Wednesday, 5th February, 1986, at 2.30 p.m.. This was to be our first date.

For the next few nights I lay awake in my cell trying to make mental preparation for my first meeting with June. *What will I say? What will we talk about? What will she think of it all?*

On the appointed day I had all my questions catalogued in my head. After the prison routine of that morning I was conducted to the visiting hall at 2.30 in the afternoon. There I met June for the first time, face to face at last.

As I had guessed from her correspondence, June was a very quiet and shy girl. I did most of the talking while she listened, smiled a lot and blushed periodically. She patiently answered my many questions about her work, her family and her church.

When visiting time was up there was a bashful 'goodbye' after which I returned to my cell and June went back to Ballinderry. Once in the cell I immediately wrote to June the longest letter I had ever written in which I told her how much I had appreciated and enjoyed her visit. I went so far as to tell her that I "really liked" her. To be truthful, I wanted to say I "loved her", but felt that would have to wait for another day.

Chapter 14

Matters Of The Heart

While we were serving the rest of our sentence in the 'conforming wings' of the Maze Prison, David and I wanted to make the best us of our time there to serve the Lord. We wondered how we might do that most effectively and be able to evangelise our whole block. We made this a matter of prayer. I believe that the Lord answered that prayer by putting His plan into our hearts and minds.

Both of us applied to join the Chief Officer's work party which would grant us a number of concessions in the prison. As Christians David and I had built up a favourable rapport with the prison authorities and were commended for our good behaviour. Various Christians, non-Christians and a few prison officers secretly came to us seeking advice on spiritual matters. We were not really surprised when we were duly accepted for the Chief Officer's work party.

Once accepted we were awarded the handsome sum of £2.56 per week. Besides this, we also had more freedom to move about the prison precincts under supervision. This allowed me more time to write longer letters to Upper Ballinderry and for David and me to attend prayer meetings and Bible study groups.

With this new liberty I decided to ask a senior prison officer for permission to place a gospel tract in every cell that he and his work party were refurbishing. The officer readily granted this permission. However, our problem was that we did not have sufficient tracts to accomplish our evangelistic project. June sent me a few tracts in each of her letters, but these were totally insufficient for what we wanted to do. Unlike zealous Christians on the outside, we could not pop into a Christian bookshop to purchase tracts.

This problem was unexpectedly solved one day after I had a conversation with a prison officer. He had previously offered to do anything for us. I, therefore, decided to take him up on his offer and asked if he could supply us with a quantity of gospel tracts. He readily consented and even though he delayed to the point that I thought he had forgotten our request, we were eventually supplied with sufficient gospel tracts to fulfil our mission.

After we obtained permission from the Chief Prison Officer we stowed our supply of literature inside a large work-box which contained the tools which were used every day by our work parties on the cells. That box became an integral part of our overall tool-kit. Some of the men on our work party used to joke about it, but none of them ever complained. When we had finished re-painting or re¬furbishing a cell, we placed a tract from our tool box on the locker for the incoming occupants of the cell.

All the prison officers knew that we had permission to engage in this evangelistic outreach. However, one day a new officer came to supervise our work party. Part of his duty was to inspect the cells after our work was finished. He had to ensure that everything was satisfactory and safe for a new batch of prisoners who would occupy the cells. This new official decided to flaunt his authority when he emerged from a cell with one of our tracts in his hand. With an obvious venomous attitude and look of contempt he crumpled our tract up in his hand and threw it up the corridor. "There is no need for that kind of stuff in there," he shouted sharply at us.

The Senior Prison Officer, the person with ultimate charge over the work-party, was carrying out another inspection two cells ahead. He heard the angry commotion in the corridor and came out to see exactly what was going on. He focussed his eyes on the screwed up tract lying on the corridor wall.

"Here! You!" he called to the junior officer. "Come here this minute and pick that up and put it back where you found it. Don't you dare throw out one of those wee books again. These boys have permission to leave them in every cell and they must stay there. Do you understand?"

The junior officer's face reddened. He stooped and picked up the crushed tract, smoothed it out as best he could and put it back on top of the locker where he had found it.

Besides this evangelical emphasis, I had another matter that was more on my heart than on my mind. It was all to do with June Thompson. After her first visit in February, 1986, I had no doubt about my feelings for her. I just wondered if she had any feelings towards me.

I began to sign off my letters with "Love from Thomas". In return June wrote me long letters between her visits, but she was shy and only spoke in short sentences when she was with me. Nevertheless, I decided it was time to try to take this relationship to the next level. I felt it would be best for both of us to have matters clarified one way or another.

Rather than startle June during one of her visits to the Maze, I decided to disclose my feeling for her in a letter. Looking back now I think I was exceedingly anxious to find out if June would even consider being my 'girlfriend'. I was conscious that this might be too big a step for a shy Christian girl like June to be prepared to become the girlfriend of a prisoner and a former terrorist.

I sat down in my cell and tried to compose the letter. I made many false starts and it certainly took me a long time to get through it. When I had finished writing this vital epistle, I read it over again and again, tweaking it here and there. At the end I felt that the letter was as good as I could ever make it. I felt I was measured and sincere in disclosing to June my personal feelings for her. I also enquired if she had any such feelings for me. I signed off the letter with "love from Tom."

Once the letter was in the post I felt the matter was now out of my hands and placed into the hands of the Lord. Nevertheless, I wondered how June would receive what I had written. *Will she write back? Will this be the end of a short, but pleasant liaison? I will have to wait, pray and see what happens.*

June dominated my every thought while I was waiting for her reply. After two days I heard a prison officer shout down the corridor, "Mail!"

I had been anxiously waiting for this call. I was first out to see if there was anything for me. I was disappointed to find there was nothing.

After two days without any reply my mind began to play tricks with me. I thought June must have been taking her time. Whether she knew it or not, she was certainly letting me stew in my own anxiety.

I began to imagine what it would be like if the relationship was over. *It was lovely while it lasted, but this is going to be the end. I have asked the Lord for guidance and maybe this is best.* All sorts of crazy thoughts crowded my mind. At last it happened. The officer called, "Mail!"

Again I was the first out to see if there was anything had arrived for me. The officer shouted again, "3-2-6 Martin".

That was my name and my prison number. My heart was thumping in rhythm with my trembling hand, but I tried to act casually. One glance at the handwriting on the envelope told me who the letter was from. I recognized instantly that it bore June's handwriting.

Rather than open the letter in the middle of a busy corridor with prisoners milling all around in the passage way, I decided I would hide the letter in my cell and then open it later on that evening when I would be alone and not likely to be disturbed. Having left the letter in the cell and gone about my prison chores, my mind was in a turmoil wondering what her reply might have been

Lock-up time finally came at half-past eight and I was left alone in my cell. After making a cup of tea I sat down and just stared at the letter which I had left propped up in the middle of the table. I resisted the temptation to open it before listening to the evening news on the radio.

Finally, at ten past nine I carefully opened the envelope. Instinct told me to look at the last page first. I wanted to know how June had signed off her letter. Half-way down the final page I discovered she had written, "All my love, June". Better still, the rest of the page was covered with "XOXOXOXOX". That told me everything I needed to know. I was so astounded that I did not know whether I should laugh or cry, stand up and shout, or sit down and sing. I then thought I should kneel down to thank God for answered prayer. Before that night was over I think I did all these, more than once.

I was thrilled to find that June said she loved me as much as I loved her and that she would be delighted to be my girlfriend. She assured me that being in prison was not a problem to her. June said she loved me for who I was and no matter where I was. Furthermore, she also said she would be very happy to wait until I was released.

I must have read that letter twenty times or more. I could hardly sleep that night with the excitement. God was so good, June was so wonderful and I was so happy.

Even though I was behind bars, I felt very secure in knowing I had a Heavenly Father who had saved me, an earthly father who cared for me and now I had a girlfriend who loved me. I was such a happy chappy.

Chapter 15

Salt In The Cells

Maintaining a Christian testimony in the Maze Prison was no easy option. As believers we had to stand up for our faith in spite of what other inmates might have said or done. This required spiritual backbone and stamina.

An example of this happened on the day a prisoner came to retrieve a soccer ball from the middle of our Bible study group on a Sunday afternoon. "Sorry, lads," he cynically and sarcastically apologised as he lifted the ball.

David and I with four other Christian prisoners had chosen the quietest corner of the exercise yard for our Bible study where we had hoped to be free from any interruptions. However, a group of lads were intent on trying to irritate us by frequently shooting the ball into the middle of our meeting. The ball came at speed and was deliberately aimed to smack one of us on the side of the ear. The unfortunate victim who was hit by this ball would be so stunned he would 'see stars' for a moment or two.

This ill-conceived ploy by these lads was an intentional provocation designed to test our Christian tolerance and forbearance. God does give grace in these circumstances, but it was not easy for men who had formerly been involved in terrorism. The natural instinct was to exact a tooth for a tooth and an eye for an eye. However, it was the grace of God that made the difference.

High standards were expected from all who professed to have had a jailhouse conversion to Jesus Christ. Even the hardest non-believers expected us not to compromise our Christian profession. Obviously we did not do tobacco, porn, drugs and avoided smutty jokes and profane or blasphemous language. We were expected to be either for Christ, or against Him. Lukewarm and half-hearted Christians did not survive for very long in the Maze.

All Christians were subjected to various insulting taunts. Some labelled us as 'Holy Joes' or 'the Chosen Few'. They jeered at us for carrying our Bibles. Every sneering gibe, every whack with the flying ball or the 'accidental' elbow in the ribs, all these were calculated to goad us into a violent or verbal reaction.

We were sad when a few weaker individuals succumbed to this relentless ridicule, but for the most part the Christians in the prison increased in number, grew stronger in spiritual growth and more confident in their witness for Christ. What these persecutors did not know was that God was at our side and was working for us.

During those difficult years I was able to draw comfort and strength from a number of sources. My blossoming friendship with June was undoubtedly a pillar of strength to me through those days.   Letters from Jean Graham, from Ballymoney, County Antrim, were also a great encouragement during my prison years.   Jean had heard about my conversion to Christ in the Maze.   She was already engaged in writing letters to prisoners, challenging unbelievers and supporting Christians.

Jean's letters were a refreshing spring of sustenance for me. They always inspired me to search the scriptures in order to send Jean an appropriate reply. With time, my letters to Jean became more like sermon outlines than chatty correspondence. I often shared with her the gleanings of our recent Bible studies. Unwittingly, these letters and my scriptural answers and exhortations were helping to develop my mind and heart for future days. Jean often told me in her letters that our mutual correspondence had also been a great blessing to her.

Despite the endless opposition from a group of unbelievers in the Maze, I also tried to keep up an active witness to the gospel during those years in prison.   A number of fellow-prisoners and prison officers came to me individually to ask for spiritual help. God reminded us that even while in prison, Christians are expected to be both salt and light. We had to keep our light shining in the darkness and make sure that we lived as salty Christians. It became evident that our presence was having an influence for good and God within the prison walls.

We tried to take every opportunity to witness to those who were genuine seekers for the truth of the gospel. One prison officer showed a sincere interest when I shared the gospel with him on a number of occasions. Initially, he wanted to know what had made such a tremendous change in my life. Every time we chatted he always seemed to have another question about God, the Bible or salvation. This gave me good opportunities to testify to him about what God had done in my life and that of my dad and of my brother David.

I could see that this man was very sincere in seeking spiritual help. I, therefore, invited him into my cell one day so we could have a talk. I was careful to leave the door open so that no-one could accuse either of us of any untoward behaviour. A few days later that same officer trusted in Jesus Christ in his own home and later came to our wing to tell us how the Lord had come into his life.

I should not leave recalling those six years in prison without paying tribute to our dad's ceaseless loyalty and faithfulness to David and me. He visited us every week for six years in spite of the many obstacles he had to surmount. He usually travelled from Lurgan to the Crumlin Road Prison or the Maze on his Yamaha motorcycle.

I remember one day he arrived absolutely soaked at the prison's visiting area. I was so taken aback and alarmed that I asked, "What happened you Dad?"

There was a smile on his face when he light-heartedly said, "It was a big lorry on the road, son. The road was completely flooded and when this big lorry sped through the flood, the spray just drenched me."

On another day he arrived at the visiting area with frost crystals sparkling on his eyebrows and the stubble of his beard. He really looked more like 'Jack Frost' than Tommy Martin on that day.

I instinctively said, "Dad, you shouldn't have come here on a day like this."

He was insistent in his reply, "I just had to come, son." Wild horses could not have kept dad back from visiting and being so attentive to David and me in those visits.

Perhaps my worst recollection about his visits was the day when father went into The Maze to visit us even though he was suffering from a very severe dose of 'flu'. When I saw him in the visiting lounge he was shivering uncontrollably. He was trying to wipe away the beads of cold sweat from his forehead in case anyone should notice he was ill. It seemed that the more he wiped his brow the more the perspiration poured out of him. I was really worried for him that day and protested, "You shouldn't have come here today, dad."

He gave me the same response as before; "I just had to come, son."

Even though David and I had broken our father's heart by our misdemeanours, yet he maintained a heart overflowing with love for us. We felt so proud of our dad because of all that he was prepared to do for us. We also were full of gratitude to God for blessing us with our dad.

Furthermore, since entering prison I had been converted, my

brother had come to the Lord and now a prison officer had professed faith in Jesus Christ. David and I had also placed a tract in every single cell in our part of the prison and we were well on our way to evangelising every cell for a second time. I was confident that God was at work in my life and through our witness.

When Paul wrote to the Philippians he recalled his time in a Philippian jail and said that the things which had happened unto him", had fallen out unto the furtherance of the gospel. In my cell I gave thought to the "the things" which had happened unto me. I smiled when I recalled what my father had forecast more than five years earlier; "It will all work out for the best. You will see."

I used to be angry with dad in those days but he still insisted, "I believe the Lord has a purpose in you coming in here."

Now I could see that dad had been right all along.

Chapter 16

The Fresh Air Of Freedom

In December 1986, I received an early Christmas box. I was informed that I would be granted my first parole from prison in four weeks time, which would be mid January, 1987. When I first heard this incredible news my initial thought was for my brother David. I wondered if he had been given parole also.

While I was excitedly rushing over to David's cell I was also afraid that he might have to remain in prison while I was on parole seeing he had to serve a longer sentence than mine. I need not have worried. David immediately confirmed the good news that he was to be paroled at the same time as me. The two of us just hugged each other. It was almost too good to be true. After over five years on the 'inside', both of us would soon be able to breathe the fresh air of freedom, even though it would only be for two days.

My eager expectation of what I would do during my two days of freedom filled every waking moment for the next four weeks. All sorts of thoughts raced through my mind; *What would it be like to be at home with our dad again? Imagine being able to walk wherever I want and whenever I wanted to. Will I still remember all the places and people after nearly four years? Have my friends changed? What will they think when they hear I have become a Christian? What will it be like to spend more time with June rather than just half-an-hour at visiting time?*

I must admit there were other times when the thought of parole caused me to be overcome with panic, apprehension and fear. Five years in prison had conditioned me to feel relatively secure in our enclosed community. During all that time I had been restricted to being acquainted with a limited number of people, all of whom were adult men.

It may be hard for outsiders to imagine what it is like to spend five years without seeing children, watching them play, hearing their laughter or even their painful cries. Also, there were no females in our lives except those we had become acquainted with on visiting days. Furthermore, I had no mother I could relate to, although June was a great blessing to me when she came on the scene half way through my time in prison. I was so looking forward to being with her.

On top of all this, every day we were supervised by a legion of uniformed guards whose primary duty was to give us orders and make sure we behaved. At the same time, we were able to cultivate friendships with some of these officers, but we were always aware that there was the distinction between "them" and "us".

I just wondered how I would cope when I would be released from this surreal society within the confines of high prison walls and if I would be able to relate to Joe Public in the free world.

At first, the prospect of these major adjustments bothered me, but little by little the anticipation and excitement of the benefits and positive aspects of parole outweighed and smothered any frightening thoughts of how I might cope.

By the time the last week before parole came round I was counting the hours until I would be walking out through the gates of the Maze. Parole was my waking thought every morning and set me in good form for the day that lay ahead. I was smiling, singing and whistling while I worked with great enthusiasm throughout the whole day. Every hour that passed hastened on that long-awaited moment.

Our dad was overjoyed when he heard that David and I were being released for two days in January. The news was an early Christmas present for him also. He could hardly believe it even though he knew it was another answer to his prayers. Like the father of the prodigal son in the Bible, these, his sons, had been lost and now they were saved; they had gone into prison on the broad road to destruction, now they were following in the footsteps of the Saviour. This caused Tommy Martin to praise the Lord.

Although dad did not want to monopolise our time at home, he did make one simple request; "If your parole coincides with a Tuesday night, maybe you would go with me to Hope United, our support group in Lurgan," he suggested.

Wanting to comply with dad's request David and I applied for parole on a Monday and Tuesday. Approval was given without any hesitation and we were to be released at ten o'clock on a Monday morning. We were expected to report back to the prison at ten o'clock on the following Wednesday morning.

The nearer we got to the magical date the less I was able to sleep. I lay awake most nights, planning and changing my plans of what I was going to do. On the night before my release I never closed an eye. I got out of bed very early that Monday morning and was washed and dressed long before anyone else had even wakened.

Precisely at ten o'clock on the parole morning David and I were driven out through main gates of the Maze Prison in a blacked out prison van. Even the drive in the van was a novelty for the last time we had been in a motorised vehicle was five years earlier when we were transferred ten miles from the Crumlin Road Jail to the Maze Prison.

When we emerged from the van two guards escorted us through another gate and out into freedom. I could hardly believe this was true and not a dream. After more than five years of incarceration we were set at liberty for the very first time. Even the guards seemed to be pleased for us. They bid us a cheery farewell with, "All the best, boys."

Once outside the prison perimeter on that crisp January morning we immediately recognised the familiar and smiling face of our dad. He was all wrapped up against the winter cold and standing in the middle of the prison car park. I am not sure if we ran to him or he ran to us, but I do remember that we were lost in each other's silent, but tight embrace as hot tears coursed down our cold cheeks.

Dad soon directed us to the car for our trip to Lurgan. The car belonged to a friend who offered to help dad out with transport for that special day.

While we chatted with dad constantly on our way home, at the same time I could not stop gazing at the beauty of the countryside even though it was a bleak January morning. I saw great beauty like I had never seen before in the leafless trees silhouetted against the grey winter sky and the bare fields stretching out into the misty and distant hills. I was also amazed at the new designs of cars and the many developments of fancy new houses and bungalows along the route to Lurgan. David and I were fascinated by it all.

Within a short while we turned into Trasna Way in Lurgan and the car rolled up to number 15. It was so good to be back home again. During our first hour at home David and I could not sit down. We searched all over the house, peering into every room and poking into every cupboard. We noticed that while some things in the house had changed, it was basically still the same familiar home we had been abruptly taken from six years earlier on that dreadful morning when the police arrested us.

Our tongues went like hand-bells as we all tried to catch up with the news and shared our experiences. Periodically the conversation was interspersed by dad exclaiming, "Praise God! I just can hardly believe all this."

We shared his sentiments.

In the afternoon David and I thought we would give dad a bit of a break by going out for a walk around the Mourneview estate. It felt so good and quite a novelty just to be able to go freely anywhere we wanted without feeling we were being watched by guards and followed by security cameras.

Later on that evening, soon after she had finished work in Lisburn, June arrived to visit us at 15 Trasna Way. This was the moment I had been waiting for and it was another unforgettable experience. For almost a year June and I had developed and deepened our relationship and grown to love each other very much. Most of our courtship had been through constant correspondence. Now for the first time, I was able to be alone with the one I loved without the restrictions of prison supervision and time limits. It was an unspeakable joy to be able to spend the whole evening with June and know that no one was going to step in and tell us our time was up.

Alas, the evening with June was all too short even though it was almost midnight before she left for her home in Ballinderry. We arranged to see each other on the following evening.

Although it was already very late David and I were so excited that we could not sleep. What was the point of sleeping when we were on parole? We did not want to waste our hours of liberty by lying in bed. There would be plenty of time for that when we got back to the Maze on Wednesday. Therefore, in the wee hours of the morning the two of us went out into the biting blackness of that January night and walked for miles around the sleeping town of Lurgan.

On Tuesday night David and I were the special guests at Hope United, the alcoholics support group in Lurgan, which dad and some of his friends attended. After he had become a Christian, dad had been very concerned for some of his former drinking buddies and wondered how he might be able to help them. Hope United had provided him with a way of doing something for these friends.

News had spread far and near that Tom and David Martin were going to say something at the Tuesday-night Hope United meeting. When we arrived there the place was packed to capacity. Many of our former friends and dad's old cronies who had followed the fortunes and misfortunes of our family, turned up for the meeting.

Our brother Colin was also there, with his girlfriend. Florence Cobb, who had been indirectly involved in me meeting up with June, was also there. Of course, June, the girl that I had come to know and love was there and sat quietly beside my dad.

Dad was not only pleased to see so many people at the meeting, but he was smiling like a Cheshire cat with the satisfaction of seeing all of his three sons in the meeting and especially knowing that his two youngest boys were Christians. His joy was full.

Characteristically, June sat silently and was secretly wondering what sort of things I was going to say in public. She already knew so much about me and how the Lord had changed my life, but she was speculating if she might learn something more and also hoping that it would not be too embarrassing.

For more than an hour the audience sat spell-bound as they listened to the wonderful things the Lord had done in our lives. We spoke of our five years in prison, of our conversions to Jesus Christ and of the Bible studies in the cells. The two testimonies that evening were clear and challenging. The theme of the message which went out to those gathered was: "If God can transform the life of three former Martin alcoholics, then He can do the same for others who had come to hear what we had to say."

After the meeting we returned to 15 Trasna Way where a crowd of family and friends crammed into dad's home. They remained talking well into the night and were quick to congratulate David and me and wish us well for our return to prison on the following morning.

After they finally left David and I were on a high and still very much awake. Instead of retiring to bed we went out for another long and late hike around Lurgan.

When Wednesday morning dawned we were exhausted, but the time had arrived to return to the Maze Prison. Although we were not permitted to take a lot of baggage back to the prison, there were no restrictions on us carrying a bag full of marvellous memories in our minds and hearts.

We had enjoyed our forty-eight hour parole so much that we were already looking forward to the next one.

I must confess that I found it a little bizarre that we were actually looking forward to seeing all our friends inside the Maze again to recount to them all that we had been able to pack into our short taste of freedom.

As we walked back through the gates to be readmitted to the prison David turned to me and asked, "Tom, what is the first thing we should do when we get back in here?"

I looked across at him and replied with a weary grin, "You can do what you like, Dave, but I am going to my bed." And I did.

Chapter 17

What Now?

Over the next year we had further paroles, which had increased both in length and in frequency. I enjoyed it immensely when the day for our parole arrived. It was always terrific to leave the Maze, but it was also terrible to have to come back and be behind bars again. Parole time only whetted our appetites for the day when we would finally be released and able to enjoy our freedom without have to return to the confined life behind high prison walls.

At long last we got the news which we had been eagerly awaiting for so long. We were informed that that our final release from the Maze was marked for Wednesday, 27th January, 1988. That date would not only mark a new beginning in our lives, but for me, 1988 would be a very momentous year.

On hearing of our release date the adrenalin began to run rapidly through our system. Both of us began to tick off the months, count the weeks and finally number the days and final hours before David and I would be able to walk out of the Maze as free men. Perhaps our excitement at times was greater than our patience. Some days time seemed to drag by so slowly and we thought that out release date would never come. However, it finally did arrive.

David was actually released one week before me. Because of my bad behaviour while I was still in the Crumlin Road Prison I had been put in solitary confinement at that time and sentenced to an extra week to my prison term. That week after David's release seemed to be the longest week of all my time behind bars. I could only imagine him being at home in Lurgan, talking with our dad and brother Colin and I was missing it all. During that long week I certainly found that the way of the transgressor was exceedingly hard.

The night before our long-awaited release I was reminded of the night before my first parole. It was another sleepless night in which I lay awake planning and changing my plans about who I would meet first and what I would say to them. Again I experienced the same adrenalin-charged sense of nervous anticipation of going home.

In the middle of the night it struck me like a bolt of thunder that I was also facing a different problem which I had not faced before when going on parole. This time I was going to say my final farewells to all my prison friends. Five years of fellowship and fraternity amongst prisoners and prison officers had created a virtual family ambience. Now I was going to leave all this behind. I knew I would greatly miss our Bible-study group. We had been a tower of strength to each other and they certainly had been a great encouragement to me since the time of my conversion. I knew I was going to miss all this and them.

When the long night of waiting was finally over, morning dawned I was ready to go. I still remember picking up a black polythene bag which contained all my earthly possessions and stepping out of my cell for the last time.

Quite a few friends had gathered in the corridor to say their last good-byes. Some shook my hand while others gave me a tight embrace as they wished me 'all the best' for the future. I found it extremely hard to say farewell to the Christians from our Bible-study group. We had all grown-up together in grace and in our knowledge of the Word of God and had forged close bonds of Christian fellowship.

"God bless you Tom," one emotional brother mumbled, echoing the sincerely-felt sentiments of others in our group, "May God richly bless you."

With these good wishes still ringing in my ears, I eventually reached the door, from where the blacked-out van transported me to the outer gate at the perimeter fence. Difficult as it might have been to leave all my friends behind, I definitely was turning my back on the Maze Prison and I had no intentions of ever going back there. I was looking forward to a whole new future in God's plan and with June Thompson at my side. I was leaving the pain of the past behind and reaching forward to the pleasures that were waiting before me.

True to form, my faithful and forbearing dad was waiting for me in the car park as he had been on each occasion I had been released for parole. Again we hugged and embraced each other and I was unashamedly grateful for all the love and care dad had showered on me during more than six imprisoned years, and this in spite of all the heartache I had caused him. Our tears flowed freely. It was as though someone had opened the flood gates and all our emotions had come tumbling out.

We stood there motionless for all of five minutes before dad broke the silence and said, "Son, let us go home."

I tossed my black bag into the boot of the car and we set off for Lurgan. By now I was more accustomed to the beautiful country side. My thoughts were more taken up with the question of what I was going to do with myself in the future. Prior to leaving the prison I had been reading in Mark's Gospel chapter 5. I took note of the instruction the Lord Jesus had given to a man out of whom He had cast a legion of demons; "Go home to thy friends, and tell them how great things the Lord hath done for thee, and hath had compassion on thee" (Mark 5:19).

After reading these words I made up my mind that on every opportunity I would endeavour to tell my friends and as many others as I could, of the great things God had done for me. I wanted to testify about the Lord Jesus Christ anywhere and at every opportunity God might give me.

However, the question still remained in my mind, *What am I going to do to fill the days and earn some money?*

I had finally gained my longed-for liberty, but I had very little money and no prospects of a job. Although I was converted and my life had been dramatically changed by the Lord, my Curriculum Vitae was less than impressive. I had been a convicted loyalist paramilitary prisoner who had served almost six years in jail. I knew that my record would not encourage many employers to come knocking at our door.

However, the Lord had already done great things for me and I knew He had not finished with me yet. Without being complacent, I was content to place my whole future into the Lord's sovereign hands. I claimed His promise from Proverb 3:5, 6; "Trust in the Lord with all thine heart; and lean not unto thine own understanding. In all thy ways acknowledge Him, and He shall direct thy paths."

Sunday, 31st January, 1988, was my first Sunday of freedom. Although we were just out of prison, David and I were asked to relate the testimony of our conversion and the transforming and preserving power of the gospel of the Lord Jesus Christ at the evening service in Lurgan Free Presbyterian Church.

The large and beautiful church was packed that night. Obviously the 'bush telegraph' had been busy and people had come from near and far to hear what David and I, two recently released prisoners, had to say. It might have been exciting and exhilarating for the congregation, but I found it to be a most humbling and yet a very thrilling experience. Humbling because so many people wanted to hear us and thrilling because the Lord had given us the opportunity to tell people about our wonderful Saviour.

It seemed to be that at the end of that service nobody wanted to go home. Dozens of people crowded around David and me. They were warm and cordial in welcoming us to their church family.

Eventually the congregation began to disperse. It was then that Robert Russell, a personal friend, came over to us and after congratulating us on the great meeting, he said, "I hope you don't mind me asking, but have you boys got a job yet? Or maybe I should ask if you want one?"

I could hardly believe what I was hearing, but I spoke up immediately, "No, we haven't got jobs yet, but we could do with one, I'm sure." I was not sure if Robert had anything in mind, but we were anxious to find employment.

Robert then went on to explain the situation more fully. "A Christian friend of mine runs a landscape gardening business and is always looking for good staff. If you are interested I could speak to him for you. Would you be keen on that sort of work?"

"We certainly would," I instantly replied. David nodded in agreement. He was in the same boat as I was. Both of us were completely broke and needed to earn some money.

Before our conversation had ended Robert assured us that he would speak with his friend with a view to securing a job for us in the near future. I realised that this was still January and it would be another two months before the first signs of spring would be evident and gardening work would begin to pick up.

Of course, my supreme thrill at being out of the Maze for good was that I could be with June. We knew that we loved each other very much, and wanted to share the remainder of our lives together. We could now start making serious plans for our shared future.

With that in mind, one of the first things we did was to go out and buy an engagement ring. We announced our engagement in February and set the date for our 'big day' in June of that same year. When else could *June* be married but in *June*.

This truly was a wonderful year. First I had gained freedom and now I had gained a wife. Our friends were delighted and dad was over the moon. Perhaps dad knew what most other people did not know, that I did not have any money. June actually had to lend me money from her savings to be able to buy her engagement ring. Nevertheless, we were deeply in love with each other and totally committed and devoted to our Lord and Saviour.

We knew that the Lord loved us and had provided for us over the years. I had no doubt He would do so again.

We did not have long to wait. It was a great day when David and I got a message to start work with Cecil Haffey Landscaping, of Portadown on Tuesday 1st March, 1988.

It was off to work we went, and we thanked God for it.

Chapter 18

All These Things

It was while I was still in prison that June and I had decided that we were meant for each other. We covenanted to pray for each other at ten thirty each evening. Soon we found that the more we prayed for each other the stronger grew the bond between us and the closer we were drawn together.

When it became clear that our relationship was destined to be permanent we asked God to guide us through the coming days. We agreed that our theme text should be the words of the Lord Jesus in the Sermon on the Mount; "Seek ye first the kingdom of God, and his righteousness; and all these things shall be added unto you" (Matthew 6:33).

Now that I was not only out of the Maze and we had become engaged, but we were still praying about our future plans and taking definite steps to make it all happen. In March, 1988, June and I became members of Lurgan Free Presbyterian Church. A week later we asked Rev. David Creane, the minister of our new church fellowship, to conduct our wedding ceremony in the church on Saturday, 18th June 1988.

A regular job with Mr Cecil Haffey's landscaping business meant I had a regular pay packet, for which I was very grateful. However, we still had a few problems. I suppose the greatest problem was that although we had planned and were eagerly looking forward to our wedding, as yet we had nowhere to live and therefore, we could not make any plans to set up our home.

Added to this, I had to think of the expense of the wedding and the honeymoon to follow. To be truthful, I wanted to give June a great day to remember, but the lack of finance was the big problem. I had come out of prison with all my worldly possessions in a black bin-liner. June had loaned me the money to buy an engagement ring and I had just started on a new job. It was hardly the best time to be planning a wedding. However, we were anxious to tie the knot as soon as possible,

We had learned to take all these matters to God in prayer. That meant praying about a home, the wedding expenses, the honeymoon and all that would follow. We stood on that promise God had already given us: "Seek ye first the kingdom of God, and his righteousness; and all these things shall be added unto you."

I remember one evening in early April, when we had plenty of plans, but nothing else, I said to June, "We will put God first in our lives no matter what happens. He has provided for us before and I am sure He will do so again,"

Although I had spoken these words I was deeply challenged in my own life to trust God to supply the "all these things. I wondered did this include a house and a wedding and would it even stretch as far as a honeymoon. I committed the matter to God day after day.

The first answer to this challenge of faith came about ten days after I had spoken to June about trusting God for our every need. After a church service in Lurgan, Matt and Linda Wylie spoke with me; "Thomas, I hope you don't mind us asking you a question," Matt began. My heart skipped a beat for I did not know what was coming. The last time somebody had spoken to me in this way resulted in me getting a job. Matt continued, "Do you and June have anywhere to live after you get married?"

I think the immediate shock caused my throat to dry up but I managed to say, "No. Not yet. We are still looking for somewhere in Lurgan."

Linda then spoke up and put a proposal to me, "My father died some time ago, and his house is still vacant. If you and June would like to use that house, which isn't all that big mind you, you can have it, rent free for at least a year."

I was dumbfounded. Many thoughts rushed through my head, *how kind of Matt and Linda. How good is the Lord.*

I blurted out my stammering, but sincere reply, Thank you very much. That will be wonderful. We will certainly take you up on your offer."

Just as I was about to walk away, Linda said softly, "And there's something else, Thomas. I would like to give June my wedding dress, if that would be all right."

I was totally speechless. God had promised to do 'exceeding abundant above all that we could ask or think.' This was certainly far beyond our imagination. The Lord was using His people to answer our prayers.

More was yet to follow. God had used His people to provide us with our first home and a wedding dress for my beautiful bride. When the friends at Lurgan Free Presbyterian Church learned that we were to have our wedding at their Church on June 18th, some of the ladies approached us one evening after a service. They wanted to know if we had anything arranged for the reception.

At that stage nothing had yet been arranged. When the ladies heard this they kindly offered, "We will put on a meal for you in the church hall after the wedding ceremony. We would like to do that for you so that you won't have a thing to worry about."

The Lord had been teaching us not to worry. Yet I had been worrying about who or how all this was going to be paid for. I asked the ladies, "What about all the expense of this? How much do you think it will cost?"

One of the ladies spoke up to reiterate what they had already said, "We already told you not to worry about a thing and we mean that. We can come to an arrangement about what will suit you later on."

All seemed to be falling into place. I was left to think about the honeymoon. I certainly discounted travelling to such exotic places as New York or Dubai. It would be more like Newcastle, County Down, which was only twenty-five miles away from

Lurgan, or Portrush in Country Antrim, more distant at more than eighty miles away.

When we looked at our financial situation, I concluded that it would take a miracle for us to have a honeymoon. I wondered if I could trust God to provide a miracle for the luxury of a honeymoon.

Some friends from the Faith Mission approached me and said, "Thomas, we heard you were getting married. Have you anything sorted out about your honeymoon?"

I had to give the same answer that I had already given about other details of our wedding, "No, not yet."

The friend then suggested, "You ought to try the Faith Mission College in Edinburgh. They have special rates for young Christian couples."

It was a good suggestion, but I did not know anybody at the Faith Mission College in Edinburgh. The only Christians I knew outside the Maze at that time were my father, June and the friends I had met at Lurgan Free Presbyterian Church.

One lady spoke up to take us a step further, "If you like, I will make enquiries about accommodation in Edinburgh," she volunteered. "And if it is free on your dates I will book it for you."

A few days later that same lady came back with the news that we could have our honeymoon in the Faith Mission College in Edinburgh, for £70.00 for the both of us for ten days. The lady then added, "I hope the price isn't too expensive."

It certainly was not too expensive. As a matter of fact, I thought it would give me something to set my sights upon for I was sure I could scrape up £70.00 for our 'big day'.

When the long-awaited wedding day arrived it was just as wonderful as we had ever wanted it to be. So many friends turned up at Lurgan Free Presbyterian Church to shower their good wishes on us. Most of the church congregation had turned out to see us exchange our vows before God and Rev. David Creane. It was a lovely and never-to-be-forgotten service. Following the ceremony in the church the ladies who had kindly offered to provide the wedding reception meal, excelled and exceeded all our wildest expectations. A great day was had by all.

Best of all, I was so happy that I had married my former 'pen pal', who soon became my best friend, then she was my sweetheart and consented to be my fiancé. Now June was my wife. We had come a long way in three and a half years and felt we were so greatly blessed to have each other.

As we had planned, we spent our honeymoon in Edinburgh where we had a wonderful time.

On our arrival home to our kindly provided rent-free home, we discovered that the whole house had been redecorated from top to bottom. We learned later that while we were in Edinburgh a work-party from the church had descended on the house and had it totally repainted and substantially refurnished in time for our return.

We were completely overwhelmed in our minds, humbled in our hearts and thankful to God for all His goodness. The Lord had provided 'all these things' for us as He had promised in Matthew 6:33.

We tearfully sank down to our knees at their new settee to thank Almighty God for His bountiful provision and for the friends He had given us. I remember saying to June, now Mrs Martin, "June, I think we should make that verse the motto for our new home."

"What verse do you mean, Thomas?   Is it 'seek ye first the kingdom of God?'" June was puzzled.

"Yes, that is a verse we have proved over these last months and we will continue to live by that principle," I said. "But that's not what I am talking about."

I helped her turn her head around and said, "Read that," drawing her attention to the embroidered fire screen which had been given to us as a wedding present.

I read the words out for June, "'As for me and my house, we will serve the Lord.'   Don't you think that would be a great motto text for our home?"

June readily agreed and read the words again; "As for me and my house, we will serve the Lord" (Joshua 24:15).

From our first evening in our first marital home we pledged ourselves to adopt Joshua's final declaration as our aim in family life. We had already proved that when we give priority in seeking the kingdom of God, He adds all that we need.

In our home the Lord Jesus Christ will not only have first place, we had made our choice to serve the Lord all the days of our lives.

Chapter 19

Time To Go Home

Now that June and I were happily married and setting up our home, it seemed that our skies were blue and we were being carried forward on the crest of the wave. However, we were soon to face some of life's down turns.

I knew that dad was not only glad to see David and me out of prison and moving on with our lives. We imagined that with this burden now lifted from his heart it would give him a new lease of life. Alas, contrary to our expectations, dad seemed to suddenly lose interest in life and his reason for living. It is not that he had lost his faith and love for Jesus Christ. It was a consequence of his advancing years.

I think we had forgotten that dad was beginning to look and feel his age. Undoubtedly our term in prison must have contributed quite a bit to his ageing process even though his indomitable spirit had kept him going during the previous seven years. Through that time he had to surmount all sorts of obstacles while trying to support us in prison.

His physical weakness and declining health helped dad discern that his earthly course was nearing completion. Although Colin, David and I visited him very regularly, yet we did not discern as early as he did that his life's work had been accomplished and the bend was approaching.

One day while I was with him at home in The Willows he was fighting for breath because of his asthma. Between gasps for air he panted out to me, "Son, I just want to get home."

Even though I knew he was at his Lurgan home, yet I perfectly understood what he meant. He wanted to leave his earthly trials behind and go to his eternal home, to be in heaven and at home with the Lord.

As I returned home to June later that evening I kept turning over in my mind what dad had said about going home to heaven. His words reminded me of the apostle Paul, who, nearing the end of his life, wrote, "For I am now ready to be offered, and the time of my departure is at hand. I have fought a good fight, I have finished my course, I have kept the faith; henceforth there is laid up for me a crown of righteousness which the Lord, the righteous Judge, shall give me on that day: and not to me only, but unto all them also which love His appearing" (2 Timothy 4:6-8).

Dad had certainly fought an uphill battle and through it all he had steadfastly kept the faith. During his last years he had fulfilled his greatest ambition; to see David and me saved and released from the Maze Prison.

For the two years following our release dad's health was steadily deteriorating. We discovered in early 1988 that in our absence dad had been making monthly visits to the doctor because of his asthma. By the end of that year he had to see the doctor almost every week. Even the slightest exertion left him battling for breath.

It was late in 1989 that our ailing father contracted pneumonia and was hospitalized for some weeks. Although he was allowed home for a short period after that, he was far too weak to do anything or go anywhere. The only thing he wanted to do was exactly what he had told me many times, he wanted to 'go home' to heaven.

God granted him his desire in February, 1990, just two years after our release. Dad fell victim to pneumonia again. My two brothers and I took it in turns to sit by his bedside in the Craigavon Area Hospital. We wanted to do everything we could for dad for we recognised that he had sacrificed so much for us and supported us throughout our troubled times. In spite of our desires, we felt helpless as we were forced to watch dad's life slowly ebb away. The wasted years of abusive drinking and the later unrelenting bouts of asthma had taken a severe toll on dad's physical body.

As I was sitting at his bedside painfully listening to dad gasp for breath I could have wept. I was recalling some of those special days in his life since his conversion; the evening he called us to his bedside and said he had something to tell us . . . the early morning when he thought the police had made a great mistake when they had roughly escorted David and me out of our house . . . the black day he had tearfully sat in the public gallery of Crumlin Road Courthouse to hear his two sons being sentenced to long jail terms . . . his six years of weekly visits to us in prison.

The long days and even longer nights of waiting and watching soon came to an end. I gazed at dad's dying form lapsing in and out of consciousness and listened to his rhythmic and shallow breathing in the oxygen mask. His battling for breath was soon to be over.

On Sunday, 25th February, 1990, dad's body finally gave up the struggle to survive and he finally did what he had wanted to do for months, he went 'home' and be with Christ, which is incomparably better.

We felt the loss of our dad, but we knew where he was and that he had gained that promised crown of righteousness.

Chapter 20

In God's Hands

During the spring of 1988 while we were in the throes of making plans and preparation for our forthcoming wedding, June and I attended the annual Easter Convention in the Martyrs Memorial Free Presbyterian Church, in Belfast. Many other friends from Lurgan Free Presbyterian Church were there, but this was the first time for me to experience anything like this.

I was thrilled to see so many Christians gathered together in the large and impressive Martyrs Church to hear the preaching of the Word of God. Considering that just two months earlier I had been meeting with four or five prisoners in a small cell to study the same Bible, this was such a contrast; two and a half thousand Christians for fellowship and Bible preaching.

The high-point of the Convention weekend for June and me was the first meeting on Good Friday night, 1st April. Dr Brian Green from London spoke with great power to a capacity congregation which listened with rapt attention. Dr Green challenged us all as he spoke from the words of the apostle Paul to the Philippians, "For to me to live is Christ, and to die is gain."

The entire thrust of his message was the necessity for the Christian to wholly and unreservedly give himself "as a living sacrifice unto God". Although he preached powerfully to more than two thousand people that night, yet his word came with personal challenge to me and to June.

At the close of the service Dr Ian Paisley made an appeal for anyone who wanted to dedicate their lives for the service of the Lord to come forward. At first I sat motionless with my head bowed in prayer. My hands were covering my face, but I could not stop tears trickling down my cheeks and through my fingers. I cared not for who saw my brokenness that night. God had spoken to me.

I slowly rose to my feet and looked down at the back of the hat on June's bowed head. I knew that she also had been touched by the Word of God. I leaned forward and whispered into her ear, "June, I am going up to the front."

When she raised her head to look up at me, I could see she also had been weeping. With a half-smile she whispered back to me, "And so am I."

Together we made our way to the front of the church while the congregation was still singing hymns of consecration. At the front we joined others as we knelt down beside each other and dedicated our lives to the service of God.

During the following week when I was back at my landscaping job, I wondered how we might be able to fulfil the vows we had made and be able to serve the Lord most effectively.

Some days later while I was going through my personal Bible reading in the Old Testament, I was arrested by five words from the instruction God gave to Joshua, after the death of Moses; "Arise, go over this Jordan" (Joshua 1:2).

The phrase seemed to jump out of the page at me. "Arise, go over this Jordan" I wondered what it might mean to me.

After pondering the matter for some time, the only conclusion that I could come to was that the Lord wanted me to step out in service for Him. Some folks at that time had suggested to me that I should consider entering the Free Presbyterian's Theological Hall, the Whitefield College of The Bible, to train for the Christian ministry.

Until I had read these words, "Arise, go over this Jordan", I had dismissed any possibility of studying for the ministry. Although I had willingly dedicated myself wholeheartedly to God, I had never ever considered myself as material for the Christian ministry or a possible candidate for a College.

I kept questioning myself, How could I, a recently-released paramilitary prisoner, with no formal education or qualification, and only a minimal amount of money, ever hope to enter a Bible College, pay the fees or become a minister of the gospel?.

At first I tried to banish any thought of Bible College and the Christian ministry from my mind. However, I could not get away from this steady and growing conviction. The Bible words kept re-echoing in my mind, "Arise, go over this Jordan."

My daily Bible reading soon took me back to Joshua. In the very first chapter the words of the Bible boldly stood out; "Be strong and of a good courage: for unto this people shalt thou divide for an inheritance the land, which I sware unto their fathers to give them. Only be thou strong and very courageous, that thou mayest observe to do according to all the law, which Moses my servant commanded thee: turn not from it to the right hand or to the left, that thou mayest prosper withersoever thou goest. This book of the law shall not depart out of thy mouth; but thou shalt meditate therein day and night, that thou mayest observe to do according to all that is written therein: for then thou shalt make thy way prosperous, and then thou shalt have good success. Have not I commanded thee? Be strong and of a good courage; be not afraid, neither be thou dismayed: for the LORD thy God is with thee whithersoever thou goest" (Joshua 1:7-9).

The last verse seemed to answer my doubts about God's call on my life, "Have not I commanded thee? Be strong and of a good courage; be not afraid, neither be thou dismayed: for the Lord thy God is with thee whithersoever thou goest." If God was calling me, then I had no more excuses to make. God had promised His abiding presence to carry me through wherever I went. He would not ask me to go anywhere, or do anything in my own strength.

Although all these deliberations were taking place prior to our planned wedding, I still shared my thoughts and God's dealing in my life with June. She had no hesitation in agreeing with me that God was directing me to Bible College. In fact, June was so keen on the idea that she wondered if she also should join me in this step so that both of us could prepare for Christian work.

After the dust had settled on the elation of our wedding, the honeymoon and settling in to our new life in Lurgan, June decided against going to Bible College. I was quite amazed to learn that just as the Lord had spoken to me, "Go over this Jordan", so God had clearly spoke to June while reading in Deuteronomy 3. In her reading June came on verses which she had never known or seen before, "Thou shalt not go over this Jordan" (Deuteronomy 3:27). This guidance was clear enough for June so she withdrew from any thought of going to the Whitefield College.

While reading on in the same chapter she came on these words, "But charge thou Joshua, and encourage him, and strengthen him: for he shall go over before this people ..." (Deuteronomy 3:28). June concluded that her place was not to be in Bible College, but rather, it would be her duty to support me, strengthen and encourage me in the work that God called me to.

Although I was convinced that I should pursue a course of study in the Whitefield College of the Bible I also discovered that the entry requirement to the College was for the candidate to have at least three '0' levels. I had never done an '0' level exam in my life and wondered how I was ever going to obtain three of them.

Although it seemed a daunting task at first, I remembered that the Lord had told me not to be afraid or dismayed. He had a job for me to do and He had promised to see me through.

Early in 1989 I did two things; firstly, I changed my job and began working as a fitter with UPVC Windows and also enrolled for night classes to study the English Language. I decided that I would attempt to obtain one '0' Level each year for three consecutive years. I would do English Language the first year, English Literature on the second year and if I could last the pace, I would attempt History in the third year.

Although it was time consuming to work at my job by day and then laborious study at night, we had also decided that we would not waste those three years. June and I pledged to serve God with all of our hearts and for all of our lives.

By this time news had spread amongst Free Presbyterian churches about my conversion in prison and how I had been able to testify of the grace of God. As a result, I was soon being invited to churches far and near to tell all that the Lord had done for me and for our family.

June and I travelled all over the country witnessing to everybody who cared to listen to us. I spoke the gospel to workmates, to neighbours, to family members and friends. I had wasted too many years for the devil in pubs and paramilitary parties. Now I wanted to spend my time serving the Lord in tract distribution and door-to-door evangelism.

Through hard graft I eventually met the stipulated standards and was duly offered a place at The Whitefield College of the Bible to commence my studies in September, 1993.

From the moment I first crossed the threshold of the College in Lawrencetown, near Banbridge, I loved college life. I had embarked on four years of intensive Bible study. I enjoyed the teachers and the teaching. In prison I had to search the scriptures, but I had never really been acquainted with systematic Bible teaching.

I also relished the times of fellowship with other Christians who were also preparing for Christian service at the Whitefield.

However, there was one matter that concerned me greatly at the beginning of my first term in the college. It was the same old matter of finance. I had already proved God's faithfulness in so many ways and had entered College with a step of faith. I had also reckoned that by the end of that year June and I would probably have saved up enough money to pay my fees.

While we were confident of reaching our aspired goal I was dreading having to tell the College authorities that we would only be able to pay my fees at the end of the year.

When I got the courage to approach them, I did go a little apologetically hoping for a sympathetic ear to which I would explain that we hoped to be able to pay my expenses sometime before the end of the year.

When I opened my mouth to mention fees I was interrupted with the announcement, "Don't worry another thing about that, Thomas. Your fees have already been paid."

I was flabbergasted. "What do you mean?" I asked. "I haven't given you anything yet."

"That's all right," I was told. "An anonymous donor has paid your fees for this year so you go on and enjoy the course"

Having my fees taken care of by some generous and anonymous well-wisher, was only the start of God's practical provision for me during my years of study. Someone else provided me with all the books I needed for the course. Added to this, there was the occasional envelope which was unobtrusively slipped to me after a meeting with a whisper, "Here you are, brother, that's for you." This helped meet my travelling expenses to and from the College.

I found a parallel to God's timely and ample provision for us highlighted in 2 Kings 25:30 where we read of King Jehoiachin; "And (he) changed his prison garments: and he did eat bread continually before him all the days of his life. And his allowance was a continual allowance given him of the king, a daily rate for every day, all the days of his life." From the day I left the prison cell until I finished my course at the Whitefield College of the Bible, we found that God always provided for us – sometimes it was just on the nick of time and with just enough to carry us through.

On 17th August, 1994, just after I had completed my first year at the Whitefield College, God blessed June and me with our first happy taste of parenthood. Our little boy, Aaron, was born. His arrival was a joyful and thrilling experience for our home.

I think that the biggest test of our faith at that time was just before Christmas, 1995. We had spent all our money in preparing for a very modest Christmas. Aaron was sixteen-months old and we had nothing to spend on Christmas presents for family or friends.

I must confess that we found it embarrassing. Our families and a whole galaxy of friends had been kindly showering us with all kinds of gifts and we could not afford to give them anything in return.

At the end of our evening devotions we were still a little perplexed about how we were going to get through Christmas. I said to June, "June, we will have to lay this before the Lord. I know He will see us through."

The days leading up to Christmas were passing by without any evident sign that God was going to supply our need. However, we were still trusting God. Christmas Day was on a Monday that year. Up until Friday night, December 22nd, although we had prayed earnestly, there was no apparent response. Until then we had a good measure of inward peace, but panic was beginning to filter in.

We went to bed that night knowing that there was only one more shopping day left until Christmas. Just before midnight we heard a rattle at our letter box followed by the sound of a car being driven away. I went to the hallway of our home where I found an envelope lying on the floor. On the envelope were written these words, "To Thomas, June and Aaron. May God bless you at Christmas."

I opened the envelope with trembling hands to find that it contained two hundred pounds in cash. Although it was left by some anonymous donor, we knew our heavenly Father had sent it.

On the next day we were able to buy presents for our family and some friends to whom we were indebted.

We could truly sing with full hearts that Christmas time, "O come let us adore Him, Christ the Lord."

Chapter 21

Help Me To Be That Man

There is nothing that brings more happiness to a home than the arrival of our offspring, our precious little children, by whom God blesses our homes. Children truly are the heart of the home. We were wonderfully blessed by God when our second son, Samuel, was born in February 1997. His arrival brought us special pleasure with a brother for Aaron who was two and a half years old at that time.

Remembering my own unhappy and distressed childhood only increased our resolve to provide a happy and secure home for our two little boys. However, our parental aspirations for a happy and secure home were somewhat threatened with a creeping sense of uncertainty. Our joy and contentment with family life was soberly tempered with the realisation that the end of my College course at the Whitefield was quickly approaching. We had no idea what was going to happen after graduation. Within a few months we would have to make some major decisions and yet we did not know of any options or opportunities in Christian ministry.

The fact that God had kept His promises in the past encouraged us to rest our future in those same promises. God had also provided our every need at each step of the way since that day when June and I had initially claimed the promise of Matthew 6:33 and pledged to put God first in everything. We could do no better than to still stand on the promises of God.

With the benefit of hindsight we can see how God's hand was guiding us through those days. But, we walk by faith and not by hindsight. Faith sees the promises without looking to the past. I am reminded of what the Psalmist said, "I had fainted, unless I had believed to see the goodness of the LORD in the land of the living" (Psalm 27:13).

During my final two years at Bible College I was invited to spend one day each week in practical ministry under the leadership of Dr John Douglas at Lisburn Free Presbyterian Church. The greater part of this work involved visitation amongst Dr Douglas's large congregation. I really enjoyed this practical experience and the blessing of working alongside such a great servant of God. Now with the summer of 1997 approaching I was contemplating saying my farewells to the Lisburn Church and the relative security of student days.

While thinking on these matters, Dr Douglas, who was also principal of the Whitefield College of The Bible, spoke to me about what I had in mind for the future. I had to confess that I was leaving it in God's hands without knowing what that might involve. It was then that Dr Douglas made a proposition to me. "I was wondering if you would consider helping me, Thomas?" he began. "As you know, I am very busy with my work here at the College and also as the minister at the Lisburn Free

Presbyterian Church. I know you have been very well accepted by the congregation there, and we in the Church would like you to join us for a year as my full-time assistant. How would you feel about that?"

Although I was bowled over, I lost no time in telling him I would feel honoured to accept the offer and have the opportunity of working with him and the church for another year. I had already established a good rapport with the people in Lisburn and this offer was far beyond any expectation I might have had. It was yet another answer to prayer.

This offer of a year of full-time ministry would also give me greater opportunity to gain experience in the preaching of the gospel and teaching the scriptures. Added to this, I would continue with the visitation of people in their homes or at hospital. I could not wait to get started.

I quickly discovered that learning the ministry is like learning to swim or drive a car. You can only learn to swim by swimming. You can only learn to drive a car by driving. It was only as I entered into the ministry that I gained experience in the delights and difficulties of the Christian ministry. Although I was under the guidance of a mature and caring senior minister, I was swimming, driving and learning the ins and outs and ups and downs of pastoral ministry. That year at Lisburn proved to be a wonderful year of learning and I was grateful for the confidence that both the elders and minister had put in me.

However, as the end of that year began to loom before us,

those same concerns and uncertainties about our future which we had faced before, began to creep up on us again.

Thankfully we did not have to entertain those concerns for very long. After a Tuesday early-morning prayer meeting in the summer of 1998 Dr Douglas again invited me to wait behind to have a chat with him.

At first I was not sure what he might want to speak about. Although I had full confidence in Dr Douglas and had enjoyed a great relationship with him, nevertheless, I was a little uneasy. I wondered if I had slipped up in some part of my ministry or if there had been some complaint about my activities or lack of them, I need not have worried. Dr Douglas's chat turned out to be very simple and satisfying, it bowled me over again. He spoke quietly and said, "The Session of the Church have decided to invite you to become my co-pastor in the work here in Lisburn. We have all been impressed with your ability and willingness in all aspects of our work during the past year and we would like you to contemplate joining us here on a more permanent basis."

I remained wide eyed as I silently listened to all that he was saying and allowing his news to sink into my mind. I was absolutely thrilled at being offered a permanent position with the church.

Dr Douglas continued, "Under this proposal we wish to put to you, I would be retained as senior minister and you would become my co-pastor, taking responsibility for much of the day-to-day running of the church."

Dr Douglas could see that I was somewhat stunned. I was so happy that the church had been satisfied with my work over the previous year. However, being invited to be a co-pastor to one of the senior ministers of the Free Presbyterian denomination and a man so learned and greatly respected, was an awesome responsibility for me.

I was suddenly startled out of my musings when after a minute, Dr Douglas continued, "We would like you to give this matter some serious consideration, Thomas. We will give you a month to make up your mind. Think about it and pray about it, and then let us know your decision. We also will be praying for you and June."

My thoughts were racing as I courteously listened to my senior minister. I had learned to respect him greatly. Under his tutelage I had learned so much from him and had grown immensely in my Christian life.

When he said that I had a month to make up my mind, my thoughts accelerated; I don't need a month to make up my mind. I could have given him an answer there and then, but I refrained from doing so. June and I had also learned that rather than accept everything that comes along, it is always best to 'pray about it'. Furthermore, I had to let June know about the proposal and find out what her opinion was.

In less than three weeks I told Dr Douglas what I easily could have told him on that Tuesday morning when he first informed me of the Session's proposal. I told him that subject to the approval of the congregation, I would willingly become his co-pastor at the Lisburn Free Presbyterian Church.

After I indicated my acceptance of this more permanent position at the Lisburn church, a congregational meeting was arranged at which the members unanimously accepted me to be their minister.

All that remained for me now was to be ordained into the ministry of the Free Presbyterian Church. The date was set for the "Ordination and Installation of Mr Thomas Martin as co-pastor of Lisburn Free Presbyterian Church" for Monday, 7th December, 1998.

When I awoke on the day of my ordination I could not help reflecting on the morning of my first parole from the Maze. Like then, my mind again was filled with anticipation and apprehension. I was excited, but I was also fearful of the unexpected. Although I wanted the future to arrive, I was also questioning my ability to cope with what lay ahead.

At the same time I could only think of how far the Lord had brought me; from the prison to the pulpit, from the misery of guilt and crime to the ministry of the gospel. What wonderful grace. What a wonderful Saviour. My heart was overflowing with gratitude. On top of all this, God had given me a wonderful wife and two lovely sons.

Before we left the house for the Ordination Service that evening June and I took turns at spending time in front of the mirror. Understandably, she looked beautiful in her new outfit. I was more taken up as to how I looked in the new clerical collar.

This was the first time I had ever worn one and I felt as if I was being choked.

My preoccupation with the clerical collar helped divert my attention from the meeting and allay my fears of my participation in it. However, the jitters soon returned when we started off from our home in Lurgan to drive to the church in Lisburn. In spite of our misgivings June and I knew that this was one of the biggest nights of our lives.

All of our relations had been invited to the Ordination Service and most of them had promised to come. The majority of our family relations were not Christians and I wondered what they would they think of it all? They, more than anyone, were acquainted with my chequered history and I am sure they found it hard to believe that one day they might see me wearing a clerical collar and much less, being ordained to the Christian ministry.

Dr Ian Paisley, Moderator of the Free Presbyterian Church, was planning to be there and would be taking part in the service.

The nearer we got to the time of the meeting the more I was besieged by all sorts of insinuations and misgivings. It was as if the devil was whispering in my ear, "What sort of a minister are you going to make?" He was casting up to me, "You were a member of the UVF and non-conforming paramilitary prisoner. How can you qualify as a preacher?" My colourful past kept flashing before me. Sweat broke around my new clerical collar and I got to the stage where I wanted to rip it off and turn around and go back home.

This was not the first time the devil had used this ploy. I had already learned that when Satan starts to insinuate and intimidate me I had to remember the throne of God and the Word of God; prayer at the throne of God and trust in the Word of God.

As we travelled to the meeting I began to talk with God (with my eyes wide open) instead of listening to the devil. I used the words of the Psalmist David in Psalm 25, "Remember not the sins of my youth, nor my transgressions: according to thy mercy remember thou me for thy goodness sake, O Lord." I repeated these words again and again.

Amazingly as we turned a bend on the road the lights of my car illuminated a sign at the side of the road; "H.M.P. Maze", it announced. I only caught a brief glance at the sign and then it was gone. However, the sign jolted my mind and helped me remember the pit from which I had been dug. Thank God the past was over. I reminded myself that the grace of God is exceeding abundant. I had already memorised the words of the apostle Paul who professed to be the chief of sinners; "I thank Christ Jesus our Lord, who hath enabled me, for that he counted me faithful, putting me into the ministry; Who was before a blasphemer, and a persecutor, and injurious: but I obtained mercy, because I did it ignorantly in unbelief. And the grace of our Lord was exceeding abundant with faith and love which is in Christ Jesus" (1 Timothy 1:12-14).

There is nothing that dispels the gainsaying of the devil like answering with the Word of God. The Bible reminds us that the devil is the father of lies, whereas God cannot lie and His word cannot be broken. I was resting on the blessed assurance that Jesus Christ had saved me by His grace.

My former life in Lurgan and those years in the Maze were all history now. I was driving forward to my new life, new challenges and a brand new ministry.

I remember taking my seat in the pulpit of Lisburn Free Presbyterian Church. I was humbled when I saw the sea of faces. So many people, some whom I recognised and others who were strangers, had come to see me being ordained as a minister of the gospel of Jesus Christ.

Free Presbyterian ministers from all over Ulster had assembled to represent their respective churches. They were also present to wish us God's blessing as we joined their ranks. Other students from the Whitefield College of the Bible were also there. For four years they had been my colleagues in the study hall. Now they wanted to encourage us as we stepped out into the ministry. I was so glad to see them.

Dozens of our friends from Lurgan Free Presbyterian Church who had supported me so practically since my release from prison, had also travelled up to Lisburn to be at the meeting. Their warm smiles and reassuring nods to me in the pulpit indicated their encouraging support.

I was glad that my brother David was there. We had been through so much together. He, more than anybody else, knew how far we had come. I was sure this night was as great a momentous occasion for him as it was for us.

The person I most esteemed in the meeting and in the whole world was the girl, the gift that God had given me, June, my wife of more than ten years. During the previous thirteen years June had been my loyal pen pal, my loyal girl-friend through difficult times and now my wife and the mother of our two sons.

Dr Ian Paisley based his sermon on the Bible text from Ezekiel 22:30; "And I sought for a man among them, that should make up the hedge, and stand in the gap before me for the land, that I should not destroy it: but I found none." In his message the veteran fundamentalist preacher highlighted how God was looking for men for His work, to stand in the gap and make up the hedge; special men, with special talents, to serve Him in special situations.

I was sure the message was challenging to all. It certainly was to me. I silently prayed that God would help me to be such a man as the preacher said God was looking for.

After Dr Paisley had delivered his message it was time to step forward and be ordained as the co-pastor of Lisburn Free Presbyterian Church.

A soft hush fell over the packed congregation as I testified of my former life in Lurgan, of my father and his conversion, of my involvement with the UVF and its disastrous consequences, of the long years in the Maze and of the night when I trusted Jesus Christ as Saviour.

I was able to speak of God's goodness to me since I had been released from prison and of God's patience with me, of how I met June and our subsequent wedding, of the call of God to Christian service, of Bible College and of how God had brought me to that very hour.

My voice began to tremble as I thanked the minister, Dr Douglas, the Session and members of the Lisburn Free Presbyterian Church for inviting me and entrusting to me, a former terrorist prisoner, the privilege of being ordained to the ministry of the Free Presbyterian Church.

My final appeal to the meeting was that God would help me to be that faithful man to stand in the gap.

Chapter 22

Maturing In The Ministry

The Apostle Paul was undoubtedly the greatest Christian who ever lived and the greatest minister of the gospel in the history of the church. He not only founded churches all over Asia Minor and Europe and wrote nearly half of the New Testament, he also established principles and practices which have been a pattern for all future ministries in the Christian church.

One of these biblical principles was communicated by Paul to Timothy; "And the things that thou hast heard of me among many witnesses, the same commit thou to faithful men, who shall be able to teach others also" (2 Timothy 2:2).

Paul certainly practiced what he preached for he was always investing in the lives and ministries of younger preachers so that they might benefit from his ministry and experience. It was for that reason Timothy and Titus worked alongside Paul before embarking on other ministries elsewhere. That same principle is still good today; every Paul should have a Timothy and every Timothy needs a mentor like Paul.

When I embarked on my ministry at Lisburn Free Presbyterian Dr Douglas certainly was my Paul. His wise counsel guided me and shaped my ministry for years to come. Right from the outset he told me that I should take the initiative to stamp my own identity and personality on the ministry at Lisburn Free Presbyterian Church. He insisted that my role was more than being an assistant to him, but as a co-minister in the work with him. He further urged me to be myself without pretence and not to ape others; to take responsibility as the minister and not to act as an assistant to him.

As good as his word, Dr Douglas gave me space and liberty to grow and develop my gifts in ministry. We alternated the weekly preaching schedule for the Sabbath Services and mid week Bible Study. Although at times I felt unworthy and somewhat overwhelmed by the awesome responsibility of the weekly demands of the work, Dr Douglas was always there to encourage and support me. Never at any time did he make me feel inferior. I could not have wished for a better mentor in the ministry.

Often after the early-morning prayer meeting on Tuesday mornings when others had returned home or gone to work, Dr Douglas called me aside into the little hut at the side of the church. There we pulled out chairs and for the next three or four hours we would discuss and pray about the ministry at the church. I learned so much in those special sessions as he shared with me from his rich experience and taught me lessons for my life. We covered everything from the use of good English grammar in preaching to good manners in the pulpit.

Dr Douglas also impressed upon me how the life of a minister can be one of solitude, being a friend to all the flock of God, but partial to none; the importance of taking an active interest in what was happening in every department of the church, but avoiding cliques and factions in the congregation. He imparted to me his methods of Bible study and precious insights into the Word of God. Those Tuesday mornings were hours well invested and they cemented a bond between us which produced rich blessings in the Lisburn church.

Not surprisingly, the church began to grow and the Lord helped me to mature in the ministry of the gospel. The discipline of constant Bible study not only helped me grow in my Christian life, it was also shaping me and my ministry. The responsibility of regular preaching in the Lisburn church alongside this man of God also helped me to develop in competence and confidence. It is generally thought that preachers do not make very good listeners, but Dr John Douglas graciously fulfilled the role of playing second fiddle to a novice like me and allowed me to grow in the ministry of the gospel.

Another quality of this wise counsellor was that he never ever pulled me aside to correct anything I might have said; although I have no doubt there were times when he might have had good reason to have done so. However, perhaps being sensitive to my humanity and lest he should crush a young preacher, he waited a few weeks and then he would gently say, "Thomas, if you can't bear what I am going to say I want you to be honest with me and tell me so."

I had learned to have confidence in Dr Douglas as a thoughtful and sympathetic mentor. I was so anxious to learn from him that he could have said anything to me. He would then recall something that had been said several weeks earlier and open it up for discussion. He did not lecture me. He listened to me as well as taking time to teach me from the Word of God. His advice and corrections were always constructive and God helped me accept and benefit from these.

After three fruitful years in the ministry at Lisburn the Session of the church decided it was time to think of building a new church, a bigger building which would have more adequate parking and better facilities. Twenty years previously the leaders of the church had wisely invested in purchasing a plot of land on the nearby Windermere Road, which was less than a mile away from its location on the Ballymacash Road.

The construction of the new church took more than a year and we were able to open the beautiful new premises to the glory of God in May 2002. We had a great day of praise as we recognised all that God had done in the years that had gone before. At the same time we were also aware that this was a new beginning for the church with new challenges for the future.

With the passing of the years Dr Douglas's role in active ministry gradually diminished. Initially, this was due to other responsibilities outside the church and then afterwards to his ill health. However, his influence and support continued to be as constant as ever.

Today the Lisburn Free Presbyterian Church is a vibrant church with a large congregation in a beautiful suite of buildings. We are grateful for teams of committed workers for all departments of the church. The Lisburn congregation has also commended other young men to the ministry of the gospel and sent out missionaries to various fields.

I benefitted greatly from the fellowship of my fellow ministers in the Free Presbyterian denomination and am indebted to them. One day in 2000 I received a telephone call from Dr William McCrea. After a few preliminary remarks he dropped a bombshell on me. He asked, "Thomas, would you be free to preach in a three-week gospel mission with Rev. John Gray and me at the Calvary Free Presbyterian Church here in Magherafelt?"

I was shocked! Although I had been giving my testimony of what God had done in my life for quite a few years and was now preaching on a regular basis, I had never taken part in an evangelistic mission. I was also taken aback that William McCrea, an experienced evangelist and popular gospel singer, should invite me to be part of an evangelistic outreach at his church. Nevertheless, even though I was somewhat diffident about having the capacity to be an evangelist, I told him I would be glad to share in the campaign with him and John Gray.

That step not only introduced one of the blessed experiences of my Christian life, it also turned out to be a turning point in my service for God. The Lord blessed us during that gospel mission. Participation night after night in leading the services, testifying and preaching with William McCrea and John Gray was most enjoyable. Twenty-five people were counselled about salvation after those meetings and the mission had to be extended for an extra week.

It was during that month of evangelistic mission that the Lord warmed my heart to evangelism. Not only was I constrained, but I developed a passion for evangelism. Within a short time other invitations started to arrive for me to conduct gospel missions in churches, in tents and in mission halls.

At first, my desire to serve God in this way was so great that I tended to accept every invitation that came my way. God graciously blessed in each of these missions and I felt the Lord was helping me; souls were saved, backsliders were restored to faith in Christ and God's people spoke of being blessed.

The Bible teaches that Christian ministers are to do the work of an evangelist. At the same time, Paul indicates that God bestows the specific gift of being an evangelist to some. Speaking of this ministry Paul wrote to the Corinthians that "… our sufficiency is of God; Who also hath made us able ministers of the new testament" (2 Corinthians 3:5, 6). I was conscious of my own insufficiency, but gradually began to discern that God had not only given me a passion for gospel preaching, but had also given me the gift and desire to be an evangelist. He was making me what He wanted me to be.

Consistent with this conviction and constraint for evangelism, it became clear that others also recognized this gift in me. Soon I was overwhelmed by invitations from churches and mission halls to conduct evangelic missions all over the country.

Before long this got out of hand. In one year I received twelve invitations for separate evangelistic missions. Obviously, it was physically impossible to accede to all these invitations while still continuing in the busy ministry at Lisburn Free Presbyterian Church. I did, however, commit myself to conduct five of these missions in that year. Even then I found this was unfair to our congregation in Lisburn. Finally, with the consent and support of the Session of our church, I agreed to limit my commitment to three evangelistic campaigns in each year.

I also had to balance my commitments to church life with responsibilities to my family. God blessed our home again on 12th July, 2000 with the arrival of our third son, Timothy. June has been a tower of strength to me at home and in the ministry and as a mother to our three boys. As a minister of the gospel I recognise that my priorities are as follows: as a person I am responsible before God, as a parent I am accountable for my family and as a pastor I am answerable to God for my ministry.

I am humbled to think that God should have reached me in a prison cell, transformed me by His grace, blessed me with a Christian wife and then entrusted me with the ministry of the gospel. Paul was so overwhelmed by what God had done in his life that he said, "And the grace of our Lord was exceeding abundant with faith and love which is in Christ Jesus."

I share the same sentiments as Paul.

Appendix

Grace In The Home

Thomas Martin's story truly is amazing; from penury to the pulpit via a prison cell. William Corbett, Thomas's newly-discovered half brother, thought the story was nothing short of miraculous. Even Aunt Eva was left shaking her head in disbelief at the transformation in the Martin family, especially in the lives of Tommy Martin's sons, Thomas and David. Friends and neighbours, Christians and non-Christians alike, who have known Thomas for years, still talk about the incredible turnabout in his life and behaviour.

Thomas's dramatic conversion, his Christian home and his development as a very effective minister of the gospel seemed to impress everyone except his estranged mother. Maureen Corbett had listened to her son tell his story, but she seemed to remain unmoved and without any vestige of emotion. Thomas could not help being struck by his mother's cold and resistant attitude to her own sons whom she had not seen for more than four decades. He could only conclude that she must have been a victim of hard and debased living during those long intermittent years.

On subsequent visits to Maureen's home Thomas was able to discern that little had changed in her life since the days in Nottingham when she and Tommy Martin indulged in drunken stupors and endless disputes. Thomas continued to avoid any reference to those haunting memories of the past. Rather, he used every opportunity to speak to his mother about the grace of God, what it had done in his life, how God had changed David's life and how his father had died in Christ. Maureen listened as respectfully as she could, but at the same time, she seemed to resist any urging from Thomas or David that she should take a similar step to become a Christian.

At the same time Thomas found he had a lot in common with his newly discovered half-brother, William Corbett. Finding out that William was a Christian greatly enhanced their relationship and meant they could enjoy good times of fellowship. Thomas felt more at ease to share with William about God's dealings in his life and how he was able to trace God's providence in leading him to find his estranged family only after his father had died.

In the course of their conversations William disclosed to Thomas that although the Martin boys had not known about the other half of Maureen's family, he and his sisters knew about the three Martin boys. He had actually heard about Thomas's conversion and life after his release from prison. William was also able to recognise God's providential design in allowing the family to be re-united in this way. Both of William and Thomas agreed that Maureen's difficult past had hardened her heart to the gospel and concluded that they needed to pray a lot for her.

Maureen Corbett's wasted life had not only robbed her of her emotions, her addiction to alcohol and cigarettes eventually took a severe toll on her health. Late in December 1996 Thomas got a phone call from William to say his mother had been admitted to the Ulster Hospital on the outskirts of Belfast. Thomas attended to Maureen at the hospital in the dual role of being her son and a Christian minister; as a son he was sorry to see his mother's life slowly ebbing away; as a minister he read the scriptures to Maureen and prayed with her during the final two weeks of her life. During this time Thomas learned that some years earlier Maureen had made a profession of faith in Jesus Christ, but this was without any subsequent change in her life style. In her final days Thomas and his brother David urged Maureen again to call on the name of Lord Jesus Christ for salvation. Sadly, there was no answer from her.

Maureen Corbett passed away in her sleep in January 1997. The last words Thomas spoke to her were, "For whosoever shall call upon the name of the Lord shall be saved" (Romans 13:10).

William Corbett and his sister asked Thomas to conduct their mother's funeral. It was a hard request for Thomas. His heart was awash with mixed emotions of sorrow and regret. Maureen's had been a sad life. Thomas was sorry that he had never known the warmth of a mother's love; the security of a good relationship with a mother and father who loved each other, that he had no happy memories of boyhood days at his mother's knee or the benefit of a mother's guiding hand during his adolescent years. He and his brothers had been robbed of all this. Now he would have to lay his mother's earthly remains in the soil.

Thomas took leave from the Free Presbyterian minister's annual week of prayer at Kilkeel to conduct the family funeral service at Maureen's home in Bangor. After that, Thomas's ministerial colleague, the Reverend Noel Hughes, conducted the Thanksgiving Service at the Belfast Crematorium.

At the end of this short service Noel Hughes pressed a button and the casket containing Maureen's remains slowly began to disappear from view. Thomas knew that this was the close of a sad chapter in his life and that of his two brothers. Both his father and mother, separated and estranged for many years in life, had now passed into the great eternity.

Returning from the funeral Thomas was able to adjust his thoughts from pondering with regret on the might-have-beens of life to the considering the reality of what God had done for him and June; what God had done for his father and his brother Dave. The blessings Thomas Martin had received since becoming a Christian far outnumbered and outweighed the disadvantages he had experienced in being a son in a dysfunctional home or having a wayward adolescence.

Thomas did not know the benefit and blessing of a mother and father's love, but God had given him June, a wife whom he truly loved and cherished. June and Thomas not only enjoyed a loving relationship, but they had been able to establish a Christian home where they recognised the supremacy and Lordship of Jesus Christ in their family. Silver and gold could never have enriched their home more than what the grace of God had done.

Aaron, Samuel and Timothy Martin, Thomas and June's three children, are the life and joy of their home. Their names were deliberately chosen. Thomas explains:

> "Aaron is our oldest boy, born in 1994. We called him Aaron to remind us of the Ark of the Covenant in the midst of Israel. We recognised the importance of having God in the midst of our home.

> Samuel our second child was born in 1996. He was so named because his name means "asked of God". We resist the temptation of shortening his name to 'Sam' because it leaves out the 'uel', the part of the name that contains the name of God. We recognised that prayer must be a vital part of a Christian home for every good and perfect gift comes from God.

> Timothy is our youngest son. He was born in 2000 and his name means "honour God". As a family we seek to honour God in everything we do.

Thomas and June endeavour to provide their sons with the warmth of love which their dad had never known, the benefit and blessing of family prayers with the security and satisfaction of a godly family. The grace of God has touched Thomas' heart and home extending to his children who profess faith in Christ.

Added to all of this, God has given to Thomas Martin the inestimable privilege of being a minister of the gospel of Jesus Christ. This was not a career that Thomas had chosen. Rather, it is a calling for which he was chosen. This vocation only magnifies the grace of God.

In the natural course of life, an ungodly and divided home does not produce godly children. On the contrary, too many children suffer because of the misdeeds and disputes of parents who too easily walk away from their marriage vows and fail in their commitment to home and family.

Conversely, being born into a Christian home does not guarantee that the children of that home will follow the faith of their father or mother. Each child needs to individually trust Jesus Christ as personal Saviour.

However, whatever background we might come from, God's grace can make a difference in any family or in the life of an individual.

The grace of God certainly made a great difference in the life of Thomas Martin.

That same grace can make a difference for you today.